NaCl Rocks! [signature] Randy Evans 2007

THE KITCHEN TABLE

chef randy evans

RECIPES | RANDY EVANS AND TEAM

PROJECT COORDINATOR | KATHRYNE CASTELLANOS

BOOK DESIGN | CHRISTY BLACKBURN

EDITOR | KRISTINE KRUEGER

PHOTOGRAPHY | JAY STEVENS

WITH SNAPSHOTS BY OUR GUESTS!

bright sky press

Box 416, Albany, Texas 76430

10   9   8   7   6   5   4   3   2   1

Library of Congress Cataloging-in-Publication Data

Evans, Randy, 1975-
The kitchen table at Brennan's of Houston / by Randy Evans ; with photographs by Jay Stevens ; foreword by Alex Brennan-Martin.
    p. cm.
Includes index.
ISBN-13: 978-1-931721-85-1 (hardcover with jacket : alk. paper) 1. Cookery. 2. Brennan's of Houston (Restaurant) I. Title.

TX714.E898 2006
641.5—dc22

                                                    2006018350

Book and cover design by Christy Blackburn

Printed in China through Asia Pacific Offset

THE KITCHEN TABLE

chef randy evans

BRENNAN'S OF HOUSTON

INCLUDES
THE KITCHEN TABLE STORY BY ALEX BRENNAN-MARTIN

THE BRENNAN FAMILY IS PASSIONATE ABOUT FOOD and Southern

hospitality, so naturally they love to talk about it! We are fortunate in that we stand on

the shoulders of giants in Creole cooking, but Brennan's of Houston has been in Houston

since 1967, and our cooking has evolved. I am often asked to describe our style of Creole

cooking. I think of what we do as "Texas-Creole" — retaining our New Orleans heritage,

but adding the best from the wealth of exciting ingredients and traditions found here.

Creativity is important in any fine restaurant, but the roots of a cuisine can easily be lost

with too much interpretation. We utilize the bounty of local artisanal products that surround

Houston. There is a real thrill when we rediscover a timeless classic that is deeply rooted

in Southern tradition, give it our own twist and reintroduce it to our guests.

As with all creative endeavors, our cooking begins and ends with people, and I am so

very proud of my staff. They are a brigade of true professionals with an overwhelming

passion for food and hospitality that sets them apart from mere cooks. Much of my

personal passion for food and hospitality goes back to my childhood here in Texas,

where every special event revolved around food, family and friends. I believe in our

own special way, we create that for our guests every day.

Our family meals always centered around seasonal products from local family farms. I

learned that the quality of the raw ingredient is as important as the guest we serve it to.

The farmer's pride in his product, along with the arduous hours spent tending it, is the

key to the true flavor of our food. Using great ingredients and skillful techniques, we

allow the grower's passion to shine through.

It is this precious labor of love that is put into each and every dish, and I hope that

you will enjoy re-creating these dishes in your home and feel the joy we do.

Most of all, my staff and I would love to visit with you. Come join us at the Kitchen

Table at Brennan's of Houston!

Bon Appétit,

Randy Evans

creating a culinary

THE KITCHEN TABLE STORY BY
ALEX BRENNAN-MARTIN

I AM OFTEN ASKED ABOUT THE ORIGIN OF OUR KITCHEN TABLE, which floods my mind with so many memories, it's a story best told from the beginning.

experience

I have been very fortunate in my life, but I most often give thanks for being born into such a remarkable family. For my generation of Brennans, being a member of a restaurant family in a city that takes its food and eating out as a contact sport has been a blessing (as well as a curse, but that's another book). The family expectation to "give back" extended beyond the restaurant. The expression "To whom much is given, much is expected" … no pressure, *really*! But the family credo also created many opportunities to express myself in unexpected ways.

For the Brennans, food, celebrations and good company have always intermingled, and every occasion became reason for a party. The sight of many of these good times was my Aunt Adelaide's home in New Orleans' Garden District. My mother, sister and I lived with her in the grand 1850s mansion that was under constant loving renovation. The first room Aunt Adelaide chose to take on was the kitchen, which came as a great

surprise to all who knew and loved her. You see, she never cooked (except filet mignon for her Yorkie, "Pud"), and no one could understand why she would begin with this room. Her motivation soon became clear — you couldn't have a good party if you couldn't serve guests!

This was no ordinary kitchen, mind you; it had no table or a single place to sit! It was designed to allow for smooth service to the grandest of affairs. And parties there were! Family, friends and special characters Aunt Adelaide collected filled our home with much "eating, drinking and carrying on," as she loved to say.

Inevitably as the evening drew to a close and the crowd began to thin, those in the know would head back to the kitchen, where the fun was just beginning. These original after-parties gave Aunt Adelaide the chance to show the staff her appreciation for another job well-done. She'd pour them wine and cocktails as other guests lingered. No one in New Orleans ever knows when to go home! We children just knew to be there, and it was during these after-parties I discovered that the real stars were in the kitchen.

I now realize the importance of my time spent at school in France. At first, it seemed like I'd been banished by my family, but it was an experience I will never forget, and I have yet to properly thank my mother, Ella Brennan. I found work in some wonderful restaurants, where I discovered the kitchen table — it had the double duty of food preparation and staff meals. These were often the creation of young apprentices earning their stripes and attempting to impress their masters. An invitation to prepare the day's meal was akin to knowing a Michelin critic just entered your dining room! These tables seemed to be the heart of the kitchen, something I hadn't seen growing up in restaurant kitchens in the States.

At Brennan's of Houston, I took my family's mandate of "giving back" very seriously, and I began to ask how I could make my mark and build on what my family had begun so long ago and nurtured through generations. Then in 1991, I encountered an unusual problem for a restaurateur: A piece of equipment near the center of the kitchen had become obsolete, and we now had extra space!

Chef Carl Walker and I began to ponder what we might do with this windfall; visions of pastry areas and new ovens danced in our heads. Then he asked me, "If you could do anything at all with this gift of space, what would it be?" Once I considered it a gift, I knew we could do better than a walk-in refrigerator!

creating a culinary experience

The many good times I'd spent at the kitchen tables of France inspired me to test the waters with Chef Carl and his staff. *Invite guests into the kitchen, into our domain? Why? What good could come of this? No one else was doing this. They would be in the way! They might get hurt!* I have seen higher-flying lead balloons! But Carl had been to some of Aunt Adelaide's parties, and he knew exactly the experience I was trying to create. So with great reservation, he agreed to proceed.

The Kitchen Table was an instant success. Word of mouth spread like wildfire. It was booked months and in some cases a year or more in advance. I've often wondered why our Kitchen Table has had such an impact. I have come to believe it's the truly unique interaction of guests

and chefs. A cook can raise his head and see the face of those he just served; the guest can catch the eye of the cook and see their passion. Perhaps it's as simple as that, as it is in all good cooking — the right blend of ingredients: people and passion.

Today our table is a far cry from the cramped corner it once was. For our 30th anniversary, 1997, we gave ourselves a new kitchen, and we designed the whole place around the Kitchen Table. It is only fitting that it has become the center of our universe — just like Aunt Adelaide's kitchen.

It's not unusual for dinner guests to wander back to the kitchen, poke their head in and then want to get "involved." Actually, this became such a frequent occurrence that we created Open Kitchen Night. During the summer, we invite our Friends of Brennan's to enjoy a cocktail, taste some of our purveyor's offerings, and mix and mingle with our team. These occasions have become the place for "foodies" in the know. This is the pure Southern hospitality my cousins and I experienced in Aunt Adelaide's kitchen. I believe she would be proud of us!

When a frequent guest shared with us his secret desire to be a chef, we invited him to spend the day in our kitchen. That single experience evolved into our Chef of the Day program, where novices work alongside our staff, learning the ropes or fine-tuning their skills. After donning their personalized chef's uniform, each apprentice learns to prepare a multicourse meal, including wine

selection. The results of their efforts are shared later in the evening with dinner in the kitchen for the Chef of the Day and their guests. As diverse as the apprentices have been, the results are always the same – a new friend for us. It is wonderful when they come back to the kitchen and introduce their party to the "guys!"

Certainly the most fortunate part of my career is that I am blessed to work with folks who are as passionate about "making great memories for our guests" as I am. The enjoyment that comes to them at the end of a particularly tough shift or after putting out a large or complex party always

amazes me. There, back in the kitchen, the folks who made it all possible are rewarded in knowing they did it better than it had been done before.

Chief among those passionate people is our Executive Chef, Randy Evans (Chef Carl stepped up as our General Manager). Randy began as a line cook in 1996 while attending culinary school. In short order, he received the highest endorsement from Carl: "This kid has it!"

Being from Southeast Texas, Chef Randy finds our Texas-Creole menu right down his alley. The flavors that flow back and forth over the Sabine River, the border between my two states, are as natural to him as the rhythms of the seasonal canning he learned as a child. While the judicious

blending of our two cultures and cuisines has long been at the heart of our cooking, our "Texas-Creole" of today has a bit more terroir and sense of place. Randy has broadened our stable of growers and artisanal purveyors and is a leader in the effort to bring grower and chef together. He is sought out by both sides for his insight and enthusiasm, and to be a spokesman for this cause in which he so deeply believes.

In these pages, you will come to know him as I have. Perhaps the world does not need another cookbook, but it most certainly would do well to step into Randy's world and in doing so, become energized by the infectious joy of a young chef with extraordinary talent doing something completely, passionately and well. ■

THE KITCHEN TABLE

At the Kitchen Table, we serve a seven-course menu

created by our chefs, featuring the bounties of the season

as well as classics from 40 years of menus. The recipes

that follow are a collection of dishes that keep our team

inspired and guests coming back. Each chapter in this

book corresponds to a course served at the Kitchen Table.

These recipes allow for you to create your own menu by

picking and choosing from the chapters. You may want

a theme dinner serving only game or seafood ... perhaps

a fresh market menu from your local farmer. I invite you

to enjoy these dishes at your kitchen table.

KITCHEN DIARIES 12

LAGNIAPPE 20

SOUP 36

SALAD 52

CHARCUTERIE 68

SEAFOOD 90

MEAT 112

CHEESE 140

DESSERT 150

OPEN KITCHEN 174

THE PANTRY 192

ONE EVENING AFTER THE
MEAL AT THE KITCHEN
TABLE, a good friend and customer, Bill Kacal, took us from the
sublime to the ridiculous. He grabbed
a marker from Chef Carl's pocket and
memorialized his appreciation on the cinder
block wall behind the table.

Before we knew it, the signatures of every other guest
who followed covered the walls, then the ceiling, then
nearby equipment, then around the corner and up
the stairs, and on just about anything and everything.
An urban legend even circulated that a customer
autographed a slow-moving employee!

A tradition had begun. Our little corner of the
kitchen became the autograph space for the many
characters who sat at the old wooden farmhouse

table with friends and helped us create an uninhibited
experience from our "jacket only" dining room of
the 1990s.

In 1994, there was little space left in our kitchen
for writing on the walls, so we turned to guest books
for diners to sign instead. The messages on the next
few pages were taken from the books that remained
after the "old Kitchen Table" was replaced with the
"new Kitchen Table" in 1998. Read on, and enjoy!

kitchen table

Houston will never be the same! We have had the culinary experience of our lives. January 1997

A toast to great food and wine and all of you who make it happen! May 1993

Thank you for letting me come into your kitchen to share your good food, fun and enthusiasm. April 1995

After many wonderful experiences at Brennan's, this has been the highlight, except for April lunch on the patio! August 1994

diaries of the kitchen table

13

I had my cake and she ate it too!

August 1994

What a wonderful time being on the inside of all that goes on at Brennan's ... and being with wonderful friends in celebration of 31 years of "wedded bliss."

July 1994

Food was unbelievable. Service, friendship even better. October 1994

I can never eat again ... nothing could compare!! October 1995

We came, we saw, we ate and ate and ate and ate and ate............! June 1995

We ate everything in the kitchen, well, not everything — we left the help alone. December 1993

This was a special night! We had a special time with our friends, Craig & Carolyn. The only problem was Carolyn embarrassed us because she ate so much!! April 1995

A "Hall of Fame" dinner ~ Great Food, Great Company. May 1993

It was wonderful, exciting and fattening! February 1993

You should see what all you can really do in the kitchen!

November 1996

As we go through life, certain events and people always stay with us. Tonight at the Kitchen Table and the staff in the kitchen has been one of those unforgettable moments. We thank you for sharing this wonderful evening with us and exposing us to great food and service.

July 1996

It was a religious experience!

March 1996

Mommy!! I'm full. July 1996

This evening places second only to our wedding day. Your waitstaff is unsurpassed, and this kitchen meal is the most unique restaurant experience I have ever experienced. Once again ... thank you for the memory.

October 1995

My taste buds have experienced their first orgasm. I'm sure they will return for another! October 1995

In the kitchen all night long and we didn't even have to wear a funny hat! August 1995

Next time we will wear our muumuus!!! June 1995

We think your food is tops. I have never eaten so much so well. November 1995

Never have we been entertained so graciously by such fine hosts in such a lovely way! July 1996

No, I am no longer hungry!

May 1995

Housing makes a difference and so does the Brennan's Kitchen Table.

January 1995

Teamwork is everything. It's not a buzzword here. I only hope that our organization runs as efficiently and effectively as does Brennan's. March 1995

Kitchen Table is great. We will never return to the main dining room. January 1995

Thanks for a bird's-eye view of your expertise. February 1997

You were all wonderful!! That personal touch means so much!

March 1997

LAGNIAPPE — "A LITTLE SOMETHING EXTRA,"

lagniappe is a gift given to a customer from a store owner. At Brennan's, we like to give a little surprise to our guests, whether it's to welcome a first-time diner or a longtime friend. The word is derived from the Spanish word *la ñapa*, meaning "something that is added." Think of it as the 13th cookie in a baker's dozen.

Lagniappe is the definition of Southern hospitality that is a cornerstone of our Kitchen Table. We invite you into our home, where we spend the majority of our time and want you to feel at home. The dishes in this chapter can be your lagniappe at a dinner party or reception. Many of these recipes can be served as an hors d'oeuvre or increased and served as an entrée.

BRENNAN'S BRUNCH HUSSARD

SMOKED CATFISH MOUSSE

SHRIMP BEIGNETS

CREOLE GRAVLAX

TEMPURA CRAB-STUFFED SQUASH BLOSSOMS

CRAWFISH MAQUE CHOUX

BRENNAN'S BRUNCH HUSSARD

Serves 8

1 recipe Marchands de Vin Sauce

8 slices Fried Green Tomatoes

½ pound Honey-Cured Bacon (recipe
  on page 71), cut into 1-inch cubes

8 quail eggs

Fresh cracked black pepper

MARCHANDS DE VIN SAUCE

5 tablespoons unsalted butter,
  divided

1 cup finely diced shittake mushrooms

½ cup finely chopped tasso ham

1 tablespoon finely chopped shallot

1 tablespoon finely chopped
  yellow onion

1 teaspoon minced garlic

½ cup red wine

¾ cup Beef or Veal Demi-Glace
  (recipe on page 201)

Salt and black pepper to taste

FRIED GREEN TOMATOES

2 small green tomatoes, sliced
  ¼ inch thick

Salt and black pepper to taste

1 egg

⅓ cup milk

1 cup all-purpose flour

½ cup yellow cornmeal

¼ cup grated Parmesan cheese

3 tablespoons chopped fresh herbs
  (oregano, thyme *and/or* parsley)

½ cup vegetable oil

FROM THE CHEF ~ What Brennan's of Houston cookbook is complete without a classic brunch dish? Even at dinner, we have requests for eggs! This recipe takes a fresh look at our family classic.

FOR THE SAUCE

Heat 1 tablespoon butter in a medium sauté pan over medium-high heat. Add mushrooms, ham, shallot, onion and garlic; sauté until onion is translucent. Add wine; cook until mixture is reduced by half, about 5 minutes. Add demi-glace; simmer for 8-10 minutes. Whisk in remaining butter, 1 tablespoon at a time, until incorporated and melted into the sauce. Season with salt and pepper. Keep warm.

FOR THE TOMATOES

Season tomato slices with salt and pepper. Blend egg and milk in a small bowl. Combine flour, cornmeal, cheese and herbs in a medium bowl. Dust tomato slices with flour mixture; dip into egg wash and dust again with flour mixture. ▶

Heat oil in a sauté pan over medium-high heat; fry tomatoes for 1-2 minutes on each side or until golden brown. Drain on paper towels.

FOR THE EGGS AND BACON

Heat a small sauté pan over medium-high heat; sear bacon cubes on all sides until bacon is crispy on the surface and hot in the center. Keep warm. Using the tip of a paring knife, pierce each quail egg at the narrow end; carefully cut a circle around the egg, creating a small lid. (Repeat for all eggs prior to frying.) Heat a lightly greased nonstick sauté pan over medium heat; fry the eggs sunny-side up, about 2 minutes.

TO PLATE

Pool a spoonful of sauce in the center of plate; top with a fried green tomato slice, bacon cube and fried egg. Garnish with a sprinkling of fresh cracked black pepper. ■

Photo on page 20

SMOKED CATFISH MOUSSE
Serves 8-10

2 pounds catfish fillets

Salt and pepper to taste

¼ cup minced red onion

1½ cups Ravigote Sauce

    (recipe on page 198)

2 tablespoons softened cream cheese

1 recipe Sweet Potato Chips

1 teaspoon minced chives

SWEET POTATO CHIPS

2 medium sweet potatoes, peeled

Vegetable oil for frying

Creole Seafood Seasoning

    (recipe on page 198)

FROM THE CHEF ~ In the South, catfish is praised for its delicate, sweet flesh. This makes for a great dip. Specialty gourmet companies even make sweet potato chips if you don't have time to make your own.

FOR THE MOUSSE

Smoke seasoned catfish fillets in a 350° smoker until cooked through, about 15 minutes. Cool in refrigerator. In a food processor, combine catfish, onion, Ravigote Sauce and cream cheese. Season to taste.

FOR THE CHIPS

Using a mandoline, slice the sweet potatoes into ⅛-inch slices. For a different look, use the ridge attachment to make gaufrette (waffle) chips. Soak chips in a bowl of water for 2 hours, changing the water twice, to ensure all of the starch is rinsed off. Drain and blot potatoes to remove any excess water.

In a fryer, heat oil to 365°. Fry chips in batches (frying time will vary depending on the amount of water and sugar in potatoes). Agitate the chips in oil to keep them from sticking together. When golden and crisp, remove potatoes to drain on a wire rack or towel-lined dish. Immediately sprinkle with seafood seasoning.

TO PLATE

Fill a pastry bag with the mousse; pipe into a small ramekin or bowl. Sprinkle with minced chives. Place sweet potato chips in a paper cone-lined mint julep cup. ■

SHRIMP BEIGNETS
Serves 18

18 shell-on Gulf shrimp (36-42 count),
    peeled and deveined (with tail left on)
Creole Seafood Seasoning to taste (recipe
    on page 198)
1 egg
2 sheets puff pastry, rolled out ⅛ inch thick and
    cut into 2½-inch rounds (one for each shrimp)
1 recipe Shrimp Boudin
1 recipe Mirliton Relish
4 cups Creole Tomato Sauce (recipe on page 199)
2 tablespoons sliced chives

SHRIMP BOUDIN

¾ pound shell-on Gulf shrimp (36-42 count),
    peeled and deveined
1½ teaspoons minced shallot
1 teaspoon minced garlic
1 egg white
1 tablespoon heavy whipping cream
2 tablespoons Louisiana hot sauce
1 tablespoon Worcestershire sauce
½ tablespoon kosher salt
½ tablespoon Creole Seafood Seasoning
½ tablespoon paprika
1½ teaspoons red pepper flakes
½ cup cooked white rice
⅛ cup cooked wild rice
¼ cup chopped green onions
1 tablespoons chopped parsley
½ tablespoon chopped fresh herbs

MIRLITON RELISH

2 mirlitons (chayote)
3 tablespoons vegetable oil, *divided*
Kosher salt and white pepper to taste

1 tablespoon minced shallots
¼ cup diced tasso ham
Creole Tomato Sauce as needed

FOR THE BOUDIN

In a bowl, combine the first 11 ingredients; mix well to distribute seasoning. Put the bowl on ice to keep cold. Slowly add the mixture to a food processor to emulsify. Fold in the rice, onions, parsley and herbs. Refrigerate until needed.

FOR THE RELISH

Peel mirlitons; cut in half lengthwise and remove seed. Lightly coat with 1 tablespoon oil; sprinkle with salt and pepper. Place on a baking sheet. Bake at 350° for 45 minutes or until tender. Cool. Cut into thick julienne slices.

In a large sauté pan, heat remaining oil. Add ham; sauté for 1 minute. Add shallots and mirlitons; sauté 1 minute longer. Season with salt and pepper. Toss with about ½ cup tomato sauce.

FOR THE SHRIMP

Season shrimp liberally with Creole seasoning. Beat egg with a little water; brush over puff pastry. Place a shrimp in the middle of each pastry, leaving tail sticking out the side if desired. Spoon about 1 tablespoon boudin over shrimp. Wrap pastry around shrimp and seal seam. Deep-fry at 365° for about 4 minutes or until cooked.

TO PLATE

Spoon the relish on small plate; top with shrimp beignet and tomato sauce. Garnish with chives. Or arrange the relish and beignets on a plate and use tomato sauce for dipping. ■ *Photo on next page*

WHETHER FROM THE GULF OF MEXICO or farmed, Texas raises more shrimp than any other state. At Brennan's, we use wild-caught Gulf of Mexico shrimp.

In the Gulf, there are four varieties. Pink shrimp are the largest and sweetest but account for little of the consumption. Royal red shrimp are found in the deepest waters. Brown shrimp, which make up 55% of all Gulf shrimp consumed, have a firm flesh and hearty flavor. Finally, white shrimp make up about 35% of Gulf shrimp consumed in the U.S. They have a firm flesh and a subtle, delicate flavor. For this reason, white shrimp is my shrimp of choice.

By using Texas shrimp, I can be certain they are wholesome and subject to regulations that verify quality and safety. Shrimp farmed in foreign countries may or may not have the standards of the U.S.

When buying shrimp, be certain of freshness by looking for firm shells that are not crushed. Once the head has black spots, the shrimp is beginning to get old. All shrimp should smell ike the sea, not smell fishy.

Shrimp are sold by count or number of shrimp per pound. So if you purchase 16-20 shell-on shrimp, there will be 16 to 20 shrimp per pound. This makes it easy to purchase for a party or special event — estimate how many shrimp each person will eat, and then you have an idea of how many pounds you will need.

No matter what type of shrimp you choose, be well informed and request that your fishmonger carry shrimp from the waters of the United States.

TexasShrimp

CREOLE GRAVLAX

1 wild salmon fillet (2 pounds), skin on and
    bones removed

2 tablespoons Absolut Peppar vodka

1 tablespoon Zatarain's liquid crab boil

4 ounces Zatarain's crab boil
    in a bag (pickling spices)

4 ounces kosher salt

4 ounces sugar

SEAFOOD BOIL POTATO SALAD

1 teaspoon Zatarain's crab boil
    in a bag (pickling spices)

1 teaspoon salt

1 teaspoon sugar

1 pound Yukon Gold creamer potatoes

2 tablespoon vegetable oil

1 recipe Seafood Boil (see page 199)

1 ear fresh sweet corn, shucked

1 large carrot, julienned

CREOLE GRAVLAX

Serves 25-30

FROM THE CHEF ~ This idea came to life at
the Grand Food and Wine Affair, a gala dinner,
where it was paired with Far Niente's Cave
Collection Chardonnay. It was a hit!

I like to serve this as an hors d'oeuvre. I take
a sliver of salmon, about ½ inch thick, and roll
it into itself. I place it on the crisp potato slice
and top with the vegetables finely chopped,
then finish with a drop of rémoulade sauce.
Note that the Creole Gravlax needs 3 days
of preparation.

1 recipe Creole Gravlax

1 recipe Seafood Boil Potato Salad

1 shallot, minced

1 head frisée, cleaned and trimmed to 2 inches
    from the leaf

¼ cup Rémoulade Sauce (recipe on page 198)

FOR THE GRAVLAX

Place salmon, skin side down, on a cheesecloth-
lined rack. Brush with vodka and liquid boil.
Grind pickling spices and combine salt and sugar;
spread over fillet, covering the thick part of the
fillet heavily. Wrap with cheesecloth. Place a
baking tray over salmon; top with a 2-pound
weight. Refrigerate for 2 days.

Rinse salmon under cold running water to remove
seasonings. Return to rack; air-dry in the refrigerator for 1 day. Slice the cured salmon paper thin. ▶

In a coffee grinder, blend the pickling spices, salt and sugar. Using a mandoline, cut potatoes into ⅛-inch slices; toss with blended seasonings and oil. Arrange the slices in a single layer on a silpat-lined baking sheet. Bake at 350° for 10 minutes or until golden brown.

In a saucepan, bring Seafood Boil to a simmer. Add corn and cook for 7 minutes or until tender; remove corncob. Strain the boil into another saucepan; return to the heat. Add carrots and cook until tender, remove from liquid. Refrigerate carrots and corn. When corn is chilled, remove kernels from cob.

TO PLATE

Toss the potatoes, carrots, corn, shallot and frisée with 2 tablespoons rémoulade sauce. Place salmon slices on a plate, forming a ring with a 3-inch center. Spoon a nest of potato salad in center of ring. ■

TEMPURA CRAB-STUFFED SQUASH BLOSSOMS

Serves 8

FROM THE CHEF ~ Squash blossoms in Texas are a sign that summer has arrived. My farmers pick the blossoms early in the morning before the heat of the day wilts the delicate blossoms.

2 tablespoons vegetable oil

1 tablespoon minced yellow onion

½ tablespoon minced celery

½ tablespoon minced red bell pepper

½ pound jumbo lump crabmeat, shells removed

Salt and black pepper to taste

1 teaspoon minced chives

4 ounces goat cheese, softened

1 tablespoon grated Parmesan cheese

8 squash blossoms

Oil for frying

1 recipe Tempura Batter

1 cup mâche

1 recipe Sweet Red Curry Vinaigrette

TEMPURA BATTER

2 cups all-purpose flour

½ cup cornstarch

¼ cup rice flour

1 tablespoon baking powder

½ tablespoon salt

1 teaspoon cayenne pepper

2½ cups cold club soda

SWEET RED CURRY VINAIGRETTE

2 teaspoons red curry paste

5 tablespoons rice wine vinegar

2 teaspoons sugar

1 teaspoon Sriracha Hot Chili Sauce

⅔ cup vegetable oil

Salt and black pepper to taste

2 scallions, finely sliced on a bias

FOR THE BATTER

Sift together the dry ingredients. Whisk in club soda, a little at a time, until the right consistency is achieved. The batter should coat the back of a spoon, but some excess batter should run off the spoon. Refrigerate for at least 1 hour before use.

FOR THE VINAIGRETTE

In a small mixing bowl, mix the curry paste, vinegar, sugar and chili sauce until well combined. Slowly whisk in oil to create a broken emulsion. Season with salt and pepper. Add scallions. Allow to rest for the flavors to marry. ▶

Heat oil in a sauté pan over medium-high heat; sauté the onion, celery and red pepper for 2 minutes. Add crab, salt and pepper; heat through. Toss with chives. Transfer to a mixing bowl; chill for 30 minutes. Fold in the cheeses, being careful not to shred the crabmeat.

Carefully peel back petals of squash blossoms to expose the stamen and pistil. Using your fingers, gently pinch off stamen and pistil. Fill center of blossoms with crab stuffing; place petals over stuffing and pinch ends of petals together to seal.

Fill a fryer or a deep pot halfway with oil; heat to 375°. Holding squash blossoms by the stem, dip into tempura batter, making sure to coat completely; let any excess batter drip off. Fry until golden brown, about 1-2 minutes, turning often to brown evenly. Remove to a paper towel-lined plate.

TO PLATE

Toss the mâche with 2 tablespoons vinaigrette; place in the center of a plate. Lay fried blossom atop the greens; drizzle a little vinaigrette over and around the blossom. Serve while still warm. ■

CRAWFISH MAQUE CHOUX WITH JALAPEÑO CORN POUND CAKE
Serves 6

FROM THE CHEF ~ Maque Choux is a great combination of the Native Americans' use of corn and the okra brought to Louisiana from Africa, mixed with the Louisiana calling card — crawfish.

6 slices Jalapeño Corn Pound Cake
1 recipe Crawfish Maque Choux
4 tablespoons butter, softened
3 tablespoons bias-cut green onions

JALAPEÑO CORN POUND CAKE
10 tablespoons unsalted butter, softened
¼ cup honey
1 cup roasted corn, puréed
2 jalapeños, roasted, peeled, seeded and diced
½ cup cornmeal
½ cup corn flour (masa)
¼ cup all-purpose flour
1 teaspoon salt
4 eggs

CRAWFISH MAQUE CHOUX
1 tablespoon vegetable oil
1 cup sliced okra (¼-inch rounds)
½ cup finely diced yellow onion
1 teaspoon minced garlic
1 cup fresh cut corn
½ cup finely diced green bell pepper
½ cup finely diced red bell pepper
1 pound fresh crawfish tail meat
1 tomato, peeled, seeded and diced
2 tablespoons Worcestershire sauce
4 tablespoons Louisiana hot sauce
Salt and black pepper to taste
½ cup cold unsalted butter, cubed ▶

In a mixing bowl with a paddle attachment, whip butter and honey on high speed for 15 minutes. Fold in the puréed corn and diced jalapeños. Sift together the dry ingredients. With mixer on low speed, add 2 eggs and half of the dry ingredients. Add remaining eggs and dry ingredients, scraping the bowl to thoroughly combine. Whip on high for 2 minutes.

Pour batter into a greased 8-inch x 4-inch x 2-inch loaf pan. Bake at 325° for 1 hour and 15 minutes or until a toothpick comes out clean. Cool for 10 minutes before removing from pan to a wire rack.

FOR THE CRAWFISH

Heat oil in a sauté pan over medium-high heat; sweat okra, onion and garlic for 2-3 minutes or until tender. Add the corn and bell peppers; cook 2 minutes longer. Add crawfish and tomato; sauté until heated through. Add Worcestershire sauce, hot sauce, salt and pepper. Remove from the heat; swirl in butter to make a creamy emulsified sauce. Adjust seasoning as needed.

TO PLATE

Slice pound cake into 1-inch slices; butter both sides. Sear cake over medium heat for 1-2 minutes on each side or until golden brown. Cut slices in half to form two triangles; place one triangle flat in middle of plate and stand up the second triangle. Spoon maque choux over cake; garnish with a sprinkling of green onions. ■

SOUP — SOUP, CONSOMMÉ, POTAGE AND STEW are a few of the names used

to describe the starting course of most formal dinners. I like to think of the soup course as the façade of a home ... it lets the outsider know what to expect inside. It sets the entire mood of a meal — simple and flavorful for a light and playful occasion, or rich and fancy for a serious or celebratory event.

The recipes in this chapter run the gamut, so be adventurous and try something new, or use them as a springboard for your own creation.

OYSTERS ROCKEFELLER

BRENNAN'S GAZPACHO

SWEET CORN
& MUSHROOM

GUMBO Z'HERBS

CHICKEN
& WATERCRESS

CRAWFISH TORTILLA

RED BEANS & RICE

SHELLING PEA & BEEF

SWEET POTATO

OYSTERS ROCKEFELLER SOUP

Serves 8-10

FROM THE CHEF ~ Instead of the classic oysters Rockefeller, we pay homage to this grand New Orleans dish with a soup. The sweetness of the celery root with the licorice from the fennel and Pernod pair well with the briny oysters.

Depending on the time of year, 48 Gulf oysters may equal 1 pint, which won't yield enough oyster liquor for this soup. You may substitute clam juice (without MSG) or purchase ½ gallon of oysters and use the rest for another recipe.

2 tablespoons vegetable oil

1 cup medium diced celeriac

1 cup medium diced fennel

½ cup medium diced yellow onion

1 tablespoon minced garlic

¼ cup Pernod liqueur

6 cups oyster liquor or clam juice

1½ cups heavy whipping cream

Sea salt *or to taste*

SOUP

1 tablespoon vegetable oil

¾ cup finely diced bell pepper

¾ cup finely diced yellow onion

¾ cup finely diced celery

48 shucked Gulf oysters

Sea salt to taste

½ teaspoon finely ground white pepper

¼ cup Pernod liqueur

¼ cup chiffonade fresh spinach

FOR THE BASE

Heat oil in a saucepan over medium heat; sweat celeriac, fennel, onion and garlic for 3-4 minutes or until translucent and tender. Flambé with Pernod. Add oyster liquor and cream. Simmer for 10-12 minutes. Season to taste. Purée well in a blender. Set aside and keep warm.

FOR THE SOUP

Heat oil in a saucepan over medium-high heat; sauté the bell pepper, onion and celery for 3-4 minutes or until translucent. Add oysters; season with sea salt and pepper. Flambé with Pernod. Add reserved base; return to a simmer.

TO PLATE

Place ½ tablespoon of spinach in each warm bowl; ladle hot soup over spinach and serve immediately. ■

Brennan's Gazpacho
Serves 10-12

FROM THE CHEF ~ Dry-packed scallops are a must ... ask your local fishmonger for them. Most scallops are packed in a solution that allows them to swell with water, giving them a rubbery texture that doesn't allow the scallop to get a beautiful brown crust when searing.

6¾ cups diced seeded tomatoes

2¼ cups diced red bell pepper

2¼ cups diced seeded peeled cucumber

1¼ cups diced red onion

Juice and zest of 1 lemon

1¾ cups tomato juice

¼ cup tomato paste

¼ cup Worcestershire sauce

¼ cup Louisiana hot sauce

2 tablespoons extra virgin olive oil

2 tablespoons minced garlic

2 tablespoons fresh thyme leaves, stemmed

½ teaspoon cayenne pepper

Kosher salt and black pepper to taste

GARNISH

½ pint yellow sweet grape tomatoes, halved

½ pint red sweet grape tomatoes, halved

1 avocado, diced

2 tablespoons minced red onion

Juice of 1 lime

2 tablespoons extra virgin olive oil, *divided*

12 dry-packed diver sea scallops (U-10 or larger)

Kosher salt and black pepper to taste

FOR THE SOUP

Combine all ingredients in a nonreactive container; cover and refrigerate overnight. Purée in a blender; strain through a medium mesh strainer. Return to container. Refrigerate until chilled. Adjust seasoning if necessary.

FOR THE GARNISH

Marinate the tomatoes, avocado and onion in lime juice and 1 tablespoon olive oil. Refrigerate until ready to serve. Heat remaining oil in a large sauté pan over high heat. Season scallops with salt and pepper; pan-sear for 2 minutes on each side.

TO PLATE

Place a 2-inch ring in the center of a chilled bowl. Fill with 2 tablespoons marinated vegetables. Slice the scallops horizontally into thirds; fan over vegetables. Ladle cold soup around the ring; gently remove ring and serve. ∎

CREAM OF SWEET CORN SOUP WITH WILD MUSHROOMS
Serves 12-16

½ cup vegetable oil

28 ears yellow corn, kernels removed
   and cobs reserved

2¼ cups chopped leeks (white
   portion only)

1 sweet onion, chopped

2 tablespoons granulated sugar

4 quarts water

5 cups heavy whipping cream

Juice of 1 lime

2 tablespoons kosher salt

½ tablespoon white pepper

1 recipe Wild Mushroom Sauté

1 tablespoon bias-cut green onions

WILD MUSHROOM SAUTÉ

3 cloves garlic, minced

2 tablespoons unsalted butter

1 pound wild mushrooms
   (chanterelle, shiitake or
   any mixture)

2 tablespoons white wine

Salt and black pepper to taste

FROM THE CHEF ~ Try this soup cold in the heat of the day, and you won't be disappointed. When serving it cold, don't reduce the soup too much. Use the strained corn mash the next time you make cornbread ... it'll add an extra punch.

FOR THE SOUP

In a large saucepan over medium heat, heat oil; sweat corn kernels, leeks and onion for 4-5 minutes or until translucent. Add corncobs and sugar; cook 2 minutes longer. Cover with water and bring to a boil. Reduce heat; simmer for 1 hour. Stir in cream; simmer 15 minutes longer. Add lime juice, salt and pepper. Remove and dispose of cobs. Purée soup with a hand blender. Strain through a fine mesh strainer. Keep warm.

FOR THE MUSHROOMS

Heat a large sauté pan over medium heat; cook garlic in butter for 1-2 minutes. Add the mushrooms and sauté for 3-4 minutes or until they release their liquid. Add wine and seasonings; cook 2 minutes longer.

TO PLATE

Place mushrooms in the center of warm soup bowls. Carefully ladle soup around mushrooms. Garnish with green onions. ∎

Gumbo Z'Herbs

Serves 6-8

FROM THE CHEF ~ The toasted brown roux makes the bitterness of the greens just melt away. Enter this recipe in your next gumbo cook-off to surprise the judges, who are likely tired of the same old seafood and sausage gumbos. Add 4 cups of pulled beef from pot roast or smoked brisket to change the entire character of this gumbo, and call it "Beef Debris Gumbo."

2 tablespoons vegetable oil

1½ cups medium diced onions

½ cup medium diced red pepper

½ cup medium diced green pepper

1 cup sliced okra, optional

2 tablespoons minced garlic

6 cups Beef Stock (recipe on page 201) or
    low-sodium beef broth, *divided*

1 tablespoon Louisiana hot sauce

1 tablespoon Worcestershire sauce

2 teaspoons Creole Meat Seasoning
    (recipe on page 198)

2 teaspoons salt

3 bay leaves

¼ teaspoon dried thyme

6 tablespoons Creole Brown Roux
    (recipe on page 202)

4 cups mixed greens (kale, turnip greens, spinach,
    mustard greens, collard greens, Swiss chard and
    parsley), torn into 1-inch pieces

2 teaspoons gumbo filé

CORNMEAL DROP BISCUITS

1 cup all-purpose flour

¼ cup cornmeal

1½ teaspoons baking powder

¼ teaspoon baking soda

½ teaspoon salt

3 tablespoons unsalted butter

½ cup milk

¼ cup buttermilk

½ cup jalapeño cheese

FOR THE GUMBO

In a heavy saucepan, heat oil to the smoke point. Sauté onions and peppers until onions are translucent. Add okra if desired and sauté 1 minute longer. Add garlic and 1 cup of broth to deglaze pan. Then add hot sauce, Worcestershire sauce, seasonings and remaining broth.

Bring to a simmer; add the roux. This will give the gumbo flavor and body; it should be thick enough to coat the back of a spoon. Return to a simmer for 5 minutes. Add greens; simmer for 1 minute to wilt. Adjust seasoning with salt and pepper.

FOR THE BISCUITS

Measure the dry ingredients into a mixing bowl. Cut in butter until very fine. Make a well in center; pour milk, buttermilk and cheese into well all at once. Mix together with a fork just long enough to incorporate. With a spoon, drop six portions onto a greased baking sheet. Bake at 325° for 18 minutes or until nicely browned.

TO PLATE

Ladle gumbo into warm bowls and top each with a biscuit; sprinkle with gumbo filé. ∎

SMOKED CHICKEN AND WATERCRESS SOUP

Serves 12-16

FROM THE CHEF ~ This soup has been in our repertoire for years, and I would be remiss not to include it in this book.

¼ cup butter

¼ cup all-purpose flour

2 tablespoons vegetable oil

1 tablespoon minced garlic

2 cups diced yellow onion

1 cup diced celery

4 bunches watercress, rinsed and chopped, *divided*

2 teaspoons kosher salt

1 teaspoon black pepper

3 quarts Chicken Stock (recipe on page 201) or
   low-sodium chicken broth

1 whole smoked chicken, skinned, boned and pulled
   or 1¼ cups smoked chicken, warmed

Additional watercress for garnish

FOR THE SOUP

In a small sauté pan over medium heat, melt butter. Stir in flour until combined; cook roux for 5 minutes. Cool before adding to hot soup. ▶

CRAWFISH TORTILLA SOUP
Serves 12-16

FROM THE CHEF ~ Here is a splendid combination of Texas spices with the crawfish of Louisiana.

2 tablespoons vegetable oil

2 cups diced yellow onions

2 cups corn

1 cup diced poblano chiles

1 cup diced red bell pepper

2 tablespoons thinly sliced garlic

1 pound fresh Louisiana crawfish tail meat

2 tablespoons Creole Seafood Seasoning
    (recipe on page 198)

1 teaspoon chili powder

1 teaspoon ground cumin

1 tablespoon Louisiana hot sauce

1 tablespoon Worcestershire sauce

3 quarts Chicken Stock (recipe on page 201) or
    low-sodium chicken broth

¼ cup chopped cilantro

½ cup vegetable oil

3 fresh corn tortillas, cut into matchsticks

Heat oil in a large saucepan over medium-high heat; sauté the garlic, onion and celery. Sweat for 3-4 minutes or until vegetables are translucent. Add three bunches chopped watercress and seasonings; wilt for 3 minutes. Add stock and bring to a boil. Add roux. Simmer for 30 minutes. Remove from the heat; stir in remaining chopped watercress. Purée with a hand blender until smooth. Stir in warm smoked chicken.

TO PLATE

Ladle hot soup into warm bowls; garnish with a tuft of watercress leaves. ∎

FOR THE SOUP

Heat oil in a large saucepan over medium-high heat. Sauté the onions, corn, chiles, bell pepper and garlic for 3-4 minutes or until tender. Add crawfish, seafood seasoning, chili powder, cumin, hot sauce, Worcestershire sauce and stock. Simmer for 30 minutes. Add cilantro and adjust seasoning.

TO PLATE

Heat oil in a large sauté pan; add tortillas. Cook over medium heat until crispy. Remove to a towel-lined plate. Ladle soup into warm bowls; garnish with tortilla strips. ∎

RED BEANS AND RICE SOUP

Serves 10-12

2 tablespoons vegetable oil

2 cups diced yellow onions

1 cup diced celery

1 cup diced bell pepper

4 cloves garlic, crushed

¼ pound tasso ham, diced

1 pound dried red beans, rinsed
    and sorted

6 quarts water

2 tablespoons Louisiana hot sauce

2 tablespoons Worcestershire sauce

2 bay leaves

1 sprig fresh thyme

1½ tablespoons kosher salt

½ teaspoon white pepper

½ tablespoon vegetable oil

½ cup cooked wild rice

½ cup finely diced tasso ham

1 teaspoon minced chives

FROM THE CHEF ~ Nothing says Louisiana like red beans and rice. I always wanted to serve it, but how in a fine dining environment? Turning it into a luxurious purée was the answer. The wild rice relish with the smoky tasso ham puts it over the top!

FOR THE SOUP

Heat oil in a large saucepan over medium-high heat; sauté the onions, celery, bell pepper and garlic for 4-5 minutes or until lightly browned. Add ham; cook 2 minutes longer. Add remaining ingredients. Bring to a simmer; cover and cook for 1½ hours or until beans are tender.

Remove from the heat; purée with a hand blender until smooth. Adjust consistency with water and adjust seasonings. If desired, strain through a medium mesh strainer.

FOR THE RELISH

Heat the oil in a small sauté pan over medium heat; cook rice and ham until heated through.

TO PLATE

Spoon relish in the center of warm bowls; ladle hot soup around it, trying to not disturb the rice. Sprinkle with chives. ■

TEXAS SHELLING PEA AND BEEF STEW

Serves 12-16

2 tablespoons vegetable oil

1 tablespoon minced garlic

½ cup diced yellow onion

1 pound beef tenderloin, cut
    into ¼-inch cubes

1 tablespoon salt

1 teaspoon black pepper

2 pints whole shiitake mushrooms,
    stems removed and dried
    (for stock), sliced

4 cups fresh shelling peas (black-
    eyed, purple hull, lady creamers
    or a mixture)

½ cup white wine

1 recipe Mushroom Stock

1 stem fresh rosemary, chopped

MUSHROOM STOCK

1 tablespoon vegetable oil

1 small yellow onion, chopped

1 rib celery, coarsely chopped

1 parsnip, coarsely chopped

½ cup white wine

3 quarts Veal Stock (recipe on page
    201) or low-sodium beef broth

1 cup dried mushroom stems

1 bay leaf

FROM THE CHEF ~ Our shelling peas come from several small farms all over Southeast Texas. My favorite is the lady creamer, a small pale yellow-green pea that is so creamy when cooked, it's easy to eat a bowlful.

FOR THE MUSHROOM STOCK

In a large saucepan, heat oil over high heat; sauté the onion, celery and parsnip for 5 minutes or until they begin to caramelize. Deglaze pan with wine. Add the stock, mushroom stems and bay leaf. Simmer for 30 minutes. Strain through a fine mesh strainer; set aside.

FOR THE STEW

Heat oil in a large saucepan over medium heat; sweat garlic and onion for 3-4 minutes or until translucent. Season beef with salt and pepper. Increase heat to high; sear beef for 2-3 minutes. Add sliced mushrooms and peas. Deglaze pan with wine. Add stock. Bring to a boil; reduce heat to low. Simmer for 35 minutes or until peas are tender. Add rosemary and cook 5 minutes longer. Adjust seasoning.

TO PLATE

Ladle hot soup into warm bowls and serve. ■

SWEET POTATO SOUP

Serves 12-16

FROM THE CHEF ~ I love the combination of sweet potatoes with the earthiness of truffles. The little addition of red curry gives the soup a spicy undertone that rounds it out.

3 tablespoons butter

1½ cups sliced leeks (white portion only)

¾ cup sliced shallots

6 cups roasted sweet potato pulp (6 medium)

3¾ quarts water

2 tablespoons salt

2 teaspoons white pepper

½ tablespoon red curry paste

1½ tablespoons honey

¾ cup packed brown sugar (maybe a little less)

1 tablespoon rice wine vinegar

2 cinnamon sticks

½ cup heavy whipping cream

Truffle oil

FOR THE SOUP

Melt butter in a large saucepan over medium-high heat; sweat leeks and shallots for 2-3 minutes or until translucent. Add the next eight ingredients. Wrap cinnamon sticks in a cheesecloth sachet; add to soup. Bring to a rolling boil; reduce heat to a fast simmer. Cook for 30 minutes. Remove cinnamon sachet. Purée soup. Adjust seasoning.

TO PLATE

Whip cream to soft peaks; add truffle oil. Ladle hot soup into warm bowls; top with a dollop of cream. Finish with a drizzle of truffle oil. ■

EDIBLE MUSHROOMS are a culinary pot of gold. There are two types — cultivated and wild. Some varieties have been cultivated for hundreds of years. They include white, crimini, portobello, oyster and shiitake.

White and crimini mushrooms are mild with a firm texture. Portobellos are simply an older crimini when harvested. Oyster mushrooms are fluted, feathery and soft brown to gray, with a delicate, mild flavor and velvety texture. Shiitakes are tan to dark brown umbrella-shaped caps; they have a rich, woody aroma with a meaty texture. Remove the stems and dry them to make mushroom stock.

Wild mushrooms are the diamond in the rough. Mushroom hunters scour the forest looking for these tasty gems. Experts at spotting these edible delights can harvest several pounds a day all season long.

Chanterelles, both golden and yellow-foot varieties, can be found from summer to winter. This mushroom is a great standard in the kitchen due to its delicately sweet taste and aroma. Part of the chanterelle family, black trumpets are hollow with flared edges resembling a trumpet.

Porcini or cèpes, harvested in spring to early summer, have a great nutty flavor and buttery texture. Remember to peel the stems before cooking.

Lobster mushrooms are named for their reddish-orange color, sweet flavor and meaty texture. They are abundant from late summer to winter.

Morel mushrooms announce spring has arrived! They're tan, yellow and black with a comb-like pointed cap; they smell of the forest and have a rich nutty flavor. Morels must be cooked. First, clean them by cutting in half lengthwise while rinsing with running water, then allow to dry.

Finally, there is the prized truffle. There are four main types: white and black winter, white and black summer. Winter truffles are the most sought-after for their flavor. The white winter truffle from Piedmont, Italy, is the most prized and expensive; its aroma has a sweet finish with a slight garlic flavor. Black winter truffles from Perigord, France, have an earthy flavor and pungent aroma. Truffles are also found in Oregon, which is gaining a reputation for its truffles at a much more affordable price.

SALAD — SALADS ARE OFTEN

SERVED in Europe after the main course to cleanse the palate. That has fallen out of fashion in the United States, where salads are eaten first. I feel salads are the expression of the season and should be served accordingly. Try to use fresh produce available at your local farmers market.

Some of the salads in this chapter are meant to enliven your taste buds, while others are meant to be the link between courses. The duck, pork and tuna salads make great warm-day entrées, especially when dining al fresco. Keep in mind that the freshest of produce is a must to ensure a true culinary experience, be it crisp greens, the ripest tomatoes or the highest grade of tuna.

TUNA NIÇOISE

HEIRLOOM TOMATO

ASPARAGUS HEARTS
OF PALM

WARM SPINACH

DUCK CONFIT BISTRO

TEXAS STRAWBERRY

TEXAS PEACH

HOMEGROWN
TOMATO SUNDAE

BERKSHIRE PORK

Tuna Niçoise Salad

Serves 4

FROM THE CHEF ~ The freshest possible tuna is a must. We fly ours in from Hawaii.

1 pound sashimi grade tuna (yellowfin *or* bluefin)

Salt and black pepper to taste

1 tablespoon Dijon mustard

2 tablespoons mustard seed

2 tablespoons olive oil

¼ cup hearts of palm, sliced

1 roasted red bell pepper, peeled, seeded and julienned

16 French beans or green beans, blanched

1 head frisée, cleaned and trimmed to 2 inches from the leaf

¼ cup Olive Tapenade (recipe on page 200)

½ cup Jackson Dressing, *divided*

2 ripe tomatoes, sliced ¼ inch thick

2 hard-boiled eggs, sliced

JACKSON DRESSING

1 egg yolk

4 tablespoons Dijon mustard

2 tablespoons minced yellow onion

2 tablespoons red wine vinegar

½ teaspoon salt

1 cup vegetable oil

2 teaspoons freshly ground black pepper

FOR THE DRESSING

In a blender or food processor, combine the egg yolk, mustard, onion, vinegar and salt. While processing, very slowly add oil until completely incorporated. Season with pepper and additional salt if needed. Store in a covered container in the refrigerator for up to 1 week.

FOR THE TUNA

Season the tuna with salt and pepper; rub with Dijon, then roll in mustard seed. Heat oil in a sauté pan over high heat; sear tuna on all sides for 1 minute. Refrigerate until serving.

TO PLATE

In a large bowl, combine the hearts of palm, red pepper, beans, frisée and tapenade; season to taste and toss with ¼ cup of dressing. Season tomatoes and eggs with salt and pepper; place in center of plate. Top with salad mixture. Slice the tuna into 16 paper-thin slices; fan four slices across each salad. Drizzle remaining dressing over tuna and around the plate. ■

Photo on page 52

Heirloom Tomato Salad

Serves 4

FROM THE CHEF ~ Heirloom tomatoes
are grown from old seed stock that vary in
flavor, size and shape. Capri Classic Blue Log
is made by Westfield Farm in Massachusetts
(see information on page 147). With a unique
blue surface, this ripened cheese adds the
classic saltiness of a blue cheese and the tang
of goat cheese to the heirloom tomatoes.

4 ripe tomatoes, sliced ½ inch thick

1 Capri Classic Blue Log, cut into ¼-inch slices

1 small sweet onion, thinly shaved

2 tablespoons extra virgin olive oil

2 tablespoons aged balsamic vinegar

Salt and black pepper to taste

Arrange tomato and cheese slices on a plate. Top
with shaved onion. Drizzle olive oil over tomatoes
and around the plate, then drizzle with balsamic
vinegar. Season with salt and pepper. ■

ASPARAGUS HEARTS OF PALM SALAD
Serves 4

FROM THE CHEF ~ I think of the fried poached egg as the crouton of the salad with a hidden surprise — the hot runny yolk.

12 cipollini onions, peeled
Olive oil
32 spears pencil-thin asparagus (3 inches long),
    blanched
4 stalks hearts of palm, halved (3-inch-long sticks)
Salt and black pepper to taste
½ cup Truffle Vinaigrette, *divided*
1 head frisée, cleaned and trimmed to
    2 inches from the leaf
4 Fried Poached Eggs
Shaved black truffles

TRUFFLE VINAIGRETTE
1 egg yolk
2 teaspoons Dijon mustard
1 tablespoon minced shallot
½ tablespoon minced truffles
3 tablespoons red wine vinegar
1 teaspoon chopped fresh herbs (thyme,
    basil and oregano)
9 tablespoons truffle oil
Salt and black pepper to taste

FRIED POACHED EGGS
1 cup flour
1 cup breadcrumbs
Salt and black pepper to taste
¼ cup milk

1 egg
1 recipe Poached Eggs (see page 202)
Oil for frying

FOR THE ONIONS
Place the cipollini onions in a small ovenproof pot; cover with olive oil. Cover and bake at 350° for 1 hour or until tender. Refrigerate until needed.

FOR THE VINAIGRETTE
In a small mixing bowl, combine the first six ingredients. Slowly whisk in truffle oil, making an emulsion the consistency of slightly thin mayonnaise. Adjust seasonings and reserve.

FOR THE EGGS
Season the flour and breadcrumbs with salt and pepper. For egg wash, whisk milk and egg in a shallow bowl. Dust poached eggs with seasoned flour, then dredge in egg wash and dust with seasoned breadcrumbs. In a fryer, heat oil to 365°. Fry eggs for 1-2 minutes or until golden brown. Egg yolk should be runny and hot. Keep warm.

TO PLATE
In center of each plate, layer asparagus spears with hearts of palm in a Lincoln log effect; leaving a 2½-inch square in the center. Season with salt and pepper; drizzle with 1 tablespoon of vinaigrette per plate. Arrange cipollini onions around asparagus. Toss frisée with remaining dressing; place over vegetables. Top each with a warm fried egg. Finish with a scattering of shaved truffles. ■

WARM SPINACH SALAD

Serves 6-8

½ cup Dijon Dressing

1 recipe Charred Wild Mushrooms

¼ cup chopped cooked bacon

½ tablespoon dry sherry

6 cups fresh spinach, stemmed

½ bunch fresh parsley, chopped

2 cloves garlic, minced

¾ cup diced yellow onion

¼ cup Dijon mustard

2 egg yolks

½ cup red wine vinegar

¼ cup sugar

Salt and black pepper to taste

2½ to 3 cups vegetable oil

CHARRED WILD MUSHROOMS

1 cup quartered stemmed shiitake
    mushrooms

1 cup torn stemmed oyster
    mushrooms

1 tablespoon vegetable oil

2 tablespoons Creole Seafood
    Seasoning (recipe on page 198)

FROM THE CHEF ~ We prepare this salad table side, allowing the aroma of the bacon to permeate the table. You can prepare whole button mushrooms in the same manner as the shiitake and oyster mushrooms. And you can use a classic herb vinaigrette instead of the Dijon dressing.

FOR THE DRESSING

In a food processor, purée the parsley, garlic and onion until smooth. Add mustard, egg yolks, vinegar and sugar; blend. Season with salt and pepper. Continue processing while slowly adding oil until emulsified to the thickness of mayonnaise. Adjust seasoning if needed.

FOR THE MUSHROOMS

Toss the mushrooms with oil and seafood seasoning in a perforated grill pan. Grill over a hot open flame for 5 minutes or until mushrooms are soft and tender. Reserve until needed. (Mushrooms can be stored in the refrigerator for up to 2 days before serving.)

TO PLATE

Heat a large sauté pan over medium-high heat. Add dressing, mushrooms and bacon; heat for 1 minute. Whisk in sherry. Remove from the heat; add spinach and toss. Serve immediately. ■

Duck Confit Bistro Salad

Serves 4

FROM THE CHEF ~ The richness of the egg yolk and sweetness of the brown sugar in the dressing balance the bitterness of the frisée. The duck confit's crisp skin makes this salad complete. Make the confit the day before so the seasonings can blend.

1 recipe Duck Confit (see page 200)

1 recipe Poached Eggs (see page 202)

2 heads frisée, cored and rinsed

1 roasted red bell pepper, peeled, seeded and julienned

¼ cup Bacon Dressing

(see page 200) (see page 202)

BACON DRESSING

¾ pound bacon

½ cup chopped onion

¾ cup prepared yellow mustard

½ cup packed brown sugar

1 tablespoon minced garlic

¼ cup red wine vinegar

1 teaspoon dry mustard

1 teaspoon black pepper

1 teaspoon dried oregano leaves

Salt to taste

1 cup vegetable oil

1 cup reserved bacon fat

FOR THE DRESSING

In a large sauté pan over medium-high heat, cook bacon until crispy. Use a slotted spoon to remove bacon to paper towels. Coarsely chop bacon; set aside. Drain and reserve fat. Add onion to pan and sweat until translucent. Lower heat; add prepared mustard, brown sugar and garlic. Simmer for 2-3 minutes.

Transfer mixture to a blender; add bacon pieces. Purée until well combined. Place in a nonreactive bowl. Refrigerate until cool, about 20 minutes. Add vinegar, dry mustard, pepper, oregano and salt. Slowly whisk in oil and bacon fat until thoroughly combined. Store in a covered container in the refrigerator for up to 1 week.

TO PLATE

In a large sauté pan over medium-high, heat 3 tablespoons of fat from the confit. Sear duck quarters, skin side down, for 2 minutes. Bake at 400° for 5 minutes or until heated through and skin is crisp. Meanwhile, reheat poached eggs in hot water until yolk runs hot, about 2 minutes. In a large mixing bowl, toss frisée, red peppers and dressing. Arrange in center of plate. Place a hot poached egg alongside. Lean hot duck quarters against greens. Serve while egg is still hot. ∎

TEXAS STRAWBERRY SALAD

Serves 4

1 baguette, cut into ½-inch diagonal slices

¼ cup butter, melted

¼ cup fresh cow's or goat's milk cheese, softened

1 teaspoon chopped fresh herbs (thyme, basil
  and oregano)

8 ounces mixed greens (arugula, endive and mâche)

¼ cup Candied Almonds

8 Texas strawberries, quartered

¼ cup Texas Strawberry Vinaigrette

TEXAS STRAWBERRY VINAIGRETTE

2 cups Texas strawberries, quartered, *divided*

1 shallot, minced

2 tablespoons rice wine vinegar

¼ cup vegetable oil

Salt and black pepper to taste

CANDIED ALMONDS

¼ cup whole almonds

1 teaspoon vegetable oil

1 cup confectioners' sugar

FOR THE VINAIGRETTE

Purée 1½ cups of strawberries with shallot and
vinegar, using a hand blender in a mixing bowl.
In a slow stream, whisk in the oil to create a
creamy emulsion. Adjust seasoning. Add the
remaining strawberries. Allow for flavors to marry
a few hours before serving.

FOR THE NUTS

Toss almonds with oil. Place on a baking sheet.
Bake at 350° for 10 minutes, stirring every 3
minutes. Toss with confectioners' sugar. Cool and
store in an airtight container until ready to use.

TO PLATE

Dip baguette slices in butter. Toast or broil until
golden brown. Combine the cheese and herbs;
spread over bread. Broil until hot and bubbly.
In a large mixing bowl, toss the greens, almonds,
quartered strawberries and vinaigrette. Arrange
on plates; top with toast. ■

TEXAS PEACH SALAD
Serves 4

FROM THE CHEF ~ The unforgettable flavors of Texas peaches have guests requesting this dish long after the season is over. Texas peaches are in season from mid-May through August.

1 baguette, cut into ½-inch diagonal slices

¼ cup butter, melted

¼ cup fresh cow's or goat's milk cheese, softened

1 teaspoon chopped fresh herbs (thyme, basil and oregano)

8 ounces mixed greens (arugula, endive and mâche)

¼ cup Candied Pecans

2 Texas peaches, peeled and diced

¼ cup Texas Peach Vinaigrette

TEXAS PEACH VINAIGRETTE

4 Texas peaches, peeled and diced, *divided*

2 tablespoons peach nectar

1 shallot, minced

2 tablespoons rice wine vinegar

¼ cup vegetable oil

Salt and black pepper to taste

CANDIED PECANS

¼ cup pecan halves

1 teaspoon vegetable oil

1 cup confectioners' sugar

FOR THE VINAIGRETTE

Purée two peaches with peach nectar, using a hand blender in a mixing bowl. Add the shallot, vinegar and remaining peaches. In a slow stream, whisk in the oil to create a creamy emulsion. Adjust

seasoning. Allow for flavors to marry a few hours before serving.

FOR THE NUTS

Toss pecans with oil. Place on a baking sheet. Bake at 350° for 10 minutes, stirring every 3 minutes. Toss with confectioners' sugar. Store in an airtight container until ready to use.

TO PLATE

Dip baguette slices in butter. Toast or broil until golden brown. Combine the cheese and herbs; spread over bread. Broil until hot and bubbly. In a large mixing bowl, toss the greens, pecans, diced peaches and vinaigrette. Arrange on plates; top with toast. ■

HOMEGROWN TOMATO SUNDAE
Serves 4

FROM THE CHEF ~ This salad was created using heirloom tomatoes from Long Meadow Ranch in Napa Valley. I used their olive oil to make ice cream instead of dressing ... drizzle the balsamic as you would hot fudge on a sundae.

4 small ripe tomatoes, each cut into six wedges
Salt and black pepper to taste
1 cup Meyer Lemon Olive Oil Ice Cream
2 tablespoons olive oil
2 tablespoons aged balsamic vinegar

MEYER LEMON OLIVE OIL ICE CREAM
6 egg yolks
1 cup sour cream
½ cup sugar
½ cup extra virgin olive oil
3 cups whole milk
Salt and black pepper to taste
Juice and zest of 2 Meyer lemons
1 ounce Charbay Meyer Lemon vodka

FOR THE ICE CREAM
In an electric mixer, beat the egg yolks, sour cream and sugar until thick and light in color. Slowly beat in oil until well combined. In a large heavy saucepan over medium heat, bring milk slowly to a soft simmer. Add a cup of hot milk to the egg yolk mixture, whisking in completely. Whisk in a second cup of milk, then whisk in the final cup of milk. Stir briskly over low heat for a few minutes. The custard will thicken slightly.

Remove from the heat; strain through a fine mesh strainer. Add salt, pepper, lemon juice, zest and vodka. Refrigerate until thoroughly cooled, at least 4 hours, but preferably overnight. Freeze in an ice cream maker according to manufacturer's instructions. Hold in freezer until needed.

TO PLATE
Season tomato wedges with salt and pepper. Place in center of plate. Top with a scoop of ice cream. Finish with a drizzle of olive oil and balsamic vinegar. Serve immediately. ■

"ACETO BALSAMICO Tradizionale di Modena," balsamic vinegar of Modena, Italy, is a condiment like no other. Aromatic with acidic undertones, it has a dark brown color that is viscous. It is a perfect balance of sweet and sour that makes it a product worth having in your kitchen.

Balsamic vinegar starts its life as cooked grape juice, or must of Trebbiano and Lambrusco grapes. The must is then naturally fermented and moved from wood aging casks to add flavor and character. Made of oak, chestnut, mulberry, cherry and juniper, the casks decrease in size from 100 liters to 15 liters. As the vinegar is aged, it is moved from these wood barrels, where it receives flavors and aromas from these different varieties of wood. Oak imparts a vanilla aroma ... chestnut darkens the vinegar ... mulberry helps in concentration ... cherry adds sweetness ... and finally juniper's sap adds a tang.

Since it is so sought-after, balsamic vinegar is regulated by the Italian government just as many of the country's wines. This regulating authority dictates that the vinegar is produced from certain grapes, aged in certain varieties of wood and produced in Modena, Italy. An expert commission of tasters also certifies the age and designation. There are two levels of quality — Affinato (fine), aged for at least 12 years; and Extravecchio (fine old), aged for at least 25 years. The aging process dictates the quality, flavor, viscosity and cost of the vinegar.

Traditionally the casks are stored in attics, where the natural atmospheric conditions of the region can act upon the vinegar. The hot summer allows for the vinegar to evaporate, concentrating the flavors. During winter, the vinegar can then react with the wood it is aged in to absorb the wood's characteristics.

Aged balsamic vinegar is extremely versatile and makes a great accompaniment. It can be used in drinks, soups and salads, with meats and paired in desserts. It is a digestif as well. With its intense flavor, a small amount will go a long way. Balsamic is best when no heat is applied to it, and when it's used at the last minute to allow for the full flavor and fragrance to show through.

BERKSHIRE PORK TENDERLOIN SALAD

Serves 4

FROM THE CHEF ~ At Brennan's, we use Berkshire pork exclusively. This pork is well marbled, which makes it a nice match with flavorful ingredients such as the grilled vegetables in this salad. The spice rub also works well with beef.

1 recipe Pork Dry Rub

1 pork tenderloin (1 pound)

3 tablespoons vegetable oil, *divided*

3 small yellow onions, peeled

2 tablespoons olive oil

Salt and black pepper to taste

1 recipe Grilled Vegetables

1 recipe Red Pepper Coulis

2 cups mixed baby greens

1 tablespoon coarsely ground black pepper

2 teaspoons salt

1½ teaspoons paprika

½ teaspoon dry mustard

½ teaspoon rubbed sage

¼ teaspoon granulated garlic

1 small sweet potato, peeled and cut
   into ¼-inch slices

1 red bell pepper, seeded and quartered

1 poblano chile, seeded and quartered

1 zucchini, bias-cut into ½-inch slices

1 yellow squash, bias-cut into ½-inch slices

Salt and black pepper to taste

¼ cup olive oil

2 tablespoons balsamic vinegar

2 tablespoons chiffonade basil

2 large red bell peppers

4 teaspoons olive oil, *divided*

1 tablespoon red wine vinegar

Salt and black pepper to taste

FOR THE PORK

Blend dry rub ingredients; sprinkle over tenderloin. Rub 1 tablespoon vegetable oil into meat. Marinate for 1-2 hours. Meanwhile, rub yellow onions with olive oil; season with salt and pepper. Wrap in foil. Bake at 400° for 45 minutes or until tender. Refridgerate until cooled. Quarter each onion lengthwise, leaving the root attached. Reserve until serving.

In a large sauté pan over medium-high heat, bring remaining vegetable oil to the smoke point. Sear tenderloin for 2 minutes on all sides. Bake at 400° for 12 minutes or until a meat thermometer placed in thickest portion of pork reads 140°. Cover and let stand for 5 minutes.

FOR THE VEGETABLES

Combine the sweet potato, bell pepper, chile, zucchini and yellow squash in a large mixing bowl; toss with salt, pepper and oil. Grill vegetables over a hot open flame, cooking on both sides until tender. Return cooked vegetables to mixing bowl and toss with vinegar and basil. Marinate for 10 minutes. ▶

Rub the bell peppers with 1 teaspoon of olive oil. Roast over an open flame, charring on all sides. Place in a small bowl; cover and let stand for 5-10 minutes. Peel pepper skin and remove seeds; roughly chop peppers. Using a hand blender, purée peppers with the vinegar, remaining oil, salt and pepper until smooth. Refrigerate until needed.

Place about ½ cup of marinated vegetables per serving in center of plate. Slice tenderloin into thin diagonal slices; fan across the vegetables. Toss the mixed greens with 2 tablespoons of coulis; place ¼ cup of greens over pork. Repeat layers of vegetables, pork and greens. Place three onion quarters around the stack on each plate. Garnish with a drizzle of red pepper coulis. ■

CHARCUTERIE — YEARS AGO, PUTTING UP AND PRESERVING

foodstuffs was a necessity for survival. Now this lost culinary art is making a comeback in the form of charcuterie, a French term meaning "cooker of meat."

Charcuterie wasn't on our menus until a trip to Commander's Palace (our sister restaurant in New Orleans) inspired me. I saw that curing meats was something that could be accomplished on a large scale. Through trial and error, we came up with several recipes we are proud to have in this book. I like to serve a mixture of meats on one plate, such as tasso ham, pancetta or torchon, paired with brioche, pickles and jelly. For some, this course is the reason for eating at the Kitchen Table.

HONEY-CURED BACON

TASSO HAM

WILD BOAR TERRINE

LAMB & ROSEMARY SAUSAGE

PANCETTA

FOIE GRAS TORCHON

SATSUMA ORANGE JELLY

PRICKLY PEAR JELLY

SATSUMA MARMALADE

PEACH PRESERVES

MAYHAW JELLY

VENISON SLIDERS

JALAPEÑO BREAD-AND-BUTTER PICKLES

the simple art of cured meats

PUTTING UP MEATS IS a centuries-old process. Before refrigeration, it was the only option of preserving food for future consumption. The "magic ingredient" for this process is salt, which removes moisture from a product and in turn deters growth of harmful bacteria. The lack of moisture in a piece of meat creates an environment that is hostile to bacteria.

The best salt to use when curing meats is kosher salt. This is where the term "kosher" comes from. The Torah, which dictates Jewish food laws, prohibits the intake of blood, so meats are soaked and salted with this coarsely grained salt to remove the blood from the meat. The coarseness of the salt crystals allows for the absorption of more moisture, meaning that more moisture can be removed without the addition of more salt.

Curing salt, sometimes called Prague Powder or InstaCure, gives cured meat that pink tint. There are two types of curing salt — sodium nitrite and sodium nitrate. Nitrites are used in meats that will eventually be cooked, while nitrates are used in dry-cured meats such as prosciutto. This salt can be purchased from butcher supply companies.

Sugar can be added to cures to help add moisture to what would otherwise be a dry piece of meat. While salt pulls water out, sugar pushes moisture in. When combined with herbs and spices, the moisture pushed in will be flavored with these ingredients. Traditionally salt is combined with sugar in a 2:1 ratio, but sugar can be used up to a 1:1 ratio, depending on the desired outcome.

When curing meat, always use the freshest and highest quality of ingredients. Most importantly, make sure your work environment is clean and keep the meats refrigerated during the curing process.

HONEY-CURED BACON
Makes 4 pounds

FROM THE CHEF ~ Honey is the perfect complement to pork. I suggest a dark amber-colored honey, but you can also substitute cane syrup, molasses or maple syrup. The ratio of salt to honey will affect the texture of the product. A ratio of 2:1 or 1:1 salt to sugar is typical. More sugar will result in a juicier product, while more salt will result in a drier product.

10 ounces kosher salt

2 ounces curing salt (sodium nitrite)

1 cup honey

1 pork belly (5 pounds)

TO CURE

Combine the salts and honey; mix thoroughly. Rub over the pork belly, making sure to cover all areas. Place in a plastic tub, skin side down. Cover and refrigerate for 10 days, overhauling (rubbing and rotating) every other day.

TO DRY

Rinse the pork with cool water and soak for 1 hour to remove excess salt. Using a bacon hook, hang in the refrigerator to air-dry for 18 hours. If you do not have room to hang the cured belly, place on a wire rack on a sheet pan on the top shelf of the refrigerator.

TO SMOKE

Start your smoker with your favorite wood (I prefer apple or cherry). Regulate the heat to reach a constant temperature of 185°. Smoke the belly until the internal temperature is 150°. Remove and cool. Evenly trim sides of bacon to form straight sides. Use trimmings in soups or sauces. Cover and refrigerate bacon for up to 1 week, or vacuum-seal and freeze for up to 1 year. ∎

Tasso Ham

Makes 10-15 pounds

2 tablespoons oil

½ large onion, chopped

1 celery rib, chopped

1 carrot, chopped

1 jalapeño pepper, chopped

¼ cup chopped ancho chiles

¼ cup chopped arbol chiles

½ cup chopped apple

1 lemon, peeled and halved

2 cloves garlic

1 bag Zatarain's Crab Boil

2 tablespoons Louisiana hot sauce

2 tablespoons Worcestershire sauce

13 cups water, *divided*

½ cup salt

¼ cup sugar

1 teaspoon curing salt (sodium nitrite)

4 cups ice

10 to 15 pounds boneless
   pork sirloin

TASSO SEASONING

2 cups Creole Meat Seasoning
   (recipe on page 198)

¼ cup dried thyme leaves

¼ cup rubbed sage

¼ cup coarse ground black pepper

2 tablespoons paprika

1 teaspoon cayenne pepper

FROM THE CHEF ~ Tasso ham is my favorite snack — served fresh out of the smoker with Mayhaw Jelly or preserves on a buttermilk biscuit or slice of brioche. This recipe is slightly different from the original found in Louisiana. Ours has a little less salt and is not as dry. To make it dry, increase the salt by ½ cup.

TO CURE

Heat oil in a large saucepan over medium heat; add the next nine ingredients and sweat for 3 minutes. Add crab boil, hot sauce, Worcestershire sauce and 5 cups water. Bring to a simmer; simmer for 30 minutes. Place salt, sugar and curing salt in a large container; strain the spicy stock into the container. Stir until salt and sugar are dissolved. Add ice and remaining water; stir until ice is melted. Once cool, place pork in the brine; cover, date and marinate in the refrigerator for 10 days.

TO SEASON

Remove the pork from the brine; drain on a wire rack in the refrigerator for at least 4 hours. Combine the seasoning ingredients; rub thoroughly over pork.

TO SMOKE

Smoke the pork on a rack at 180° until the internal temperature is 155°. Remove to a wire rack; refrigerate, uncovered, for 1 day to form a crust. Cover and refrigerate for up to 1 week, or vacuum-seal and freeze. ∎

Wild Boar Terrine

Makes 18 slices

FROM THE CHEF ~ You can use venison or all
pork instead of wild boar to make this terrine.

3¾ teaspoons salt

1 tablespoon Creole Meat Seasoning (recipe
   on page 198)

1 tablespoon chopped fresh herbs

1 teaspoon black pepper

½ teaspoon dried oregano

¼ teaspoon dried thyme

⅛ teaspoon curing salt (sodium nitrite)

1¼ pounds wild boar, cut into ½-inch cubes

1 pound pork butt, cut into ½-inch cubes

½ pound pork fat, cut into ½-inch cubes

2 egg whites

1 tablespoon heavy whipping cream

¼ cup red wine

14 strips bacon, *divided**

⅓ cup dried cherries

¼ cup green peppercorns

TO BLEND

In a large mixing bowl, combine the first seven
ingredients and blend thoroughly. Add ice-cold
cubed meat and fat. Mix in the egg whites, cream
and wine. Cover and refrigerate for 30 minutes.
Fill another large mixing bowl with ice water;
place all grinding equipment in bowl. (If the
blade, plates or worm are not ice cold, they could
heat up due to the friction during grinding. If
this happens, the fat will melt and hinder the
emulsification process.) After the equipment and
meat have been chilled for 30 minutes, begin the
grinding process.

TO GRIND

Fit grinder with a coarse grinding plate. Feed
seasoned cubes of meat into the grinder. Place a
mixing bowl resting in an ice-water bath under
the grinding plates. Grind all meat into the chilled
mixing bowl. Remove bowl from ice-water bath
and replace with first bowl used to marinate
the cubed meat; mix ground meat. Feed the
ground meat through the grinder again to assure
emulsification. Mix in cherries and peppercorns
by hand. Form one patty and cook in a small sauté
pan over medium heat until cooked through; taste
to check for seasoning and adjust if necessary.

TO FILL

Line a 1½-foot sheet of plastic wrap with 11
strips of bacon, arranged with edges overlapping
each other. Cover with another sheet of plastic
wrap; roll bacon with a rolling pin. Line a terrine
mold (1½-quart capacity) with the bacon. Roll
remaining bacon strips in the same manner; place
two pieces on one end of terrine and the other two
on the opposite end, hanging off the ends of the
terrine. Pack filling firmly into the bacon-lined
terrine. Fold the bacon over the top of the terrine
and tuck between the bacon and the terrine.
Place the lid on the terrine.

TO BAKE

Place terrine in a high-sided baking dish; add hot
water to baking dish until it's halfway up the sides
of terrine. Bake at 300° for 1½ to 2 hours or until
internal temperature reaches 155°. Remove from
the oven and allow to rest for 30 minutes. Remove
lid and place terrine in refrigerator. After 1 hour,
place a heavy foil-wrapped block of wood atop the
terrine; press overnight to compress the paté, ▶

charcuterie

which will enhance its texture. The terrine may be wrapped in plastic and refrigerated for up to 5 days, or vacuum-sealed and frozen for up to 6 months.

Note: The number of bacon strips may vary, depending on the size of your pan. You need enough to line the pan, plus four strips for the ends. When lining the pan, place the strips perpendicular to the pan (not parallel on the bottom); the overlapping edges of bacon are then folded over the meat once it's packed into the terrine. The end edges need to be very long, not half a piece of bacon. ■

Photo on page 75

LAMB AND ROSEMARY SAUSAGE
Makes 7 pounds

FROM THE CHEF ~ The robust flavor of rosemary pairs perfectly with lamb. When making sausage, by using the same ratio of lean meat to fat, you can let your imagination come up with never-ending combinations. Change the garnishes, herbs or even the spices, but keep the salt ratio the same to the meat.

¼ cup chopped fresh rosemary

2 tablespoons Creole Meat
   Seasoning (recipe on page 198)

2 tablespoons kosher salt

½ tablespoon black pepper

½ tablespoon mustard powder

¾ teaspoon granulated onion

¼ teaspoon curing salt
   (sodium nitrite)

3½ pounds lamb shoulder, cut into ½-inch cubes

2½ pounds pork butt, cut into ½-inch cubes

½ pound pork fat, cut into ½-inch cubes

2 tablespoons roasted garlic

2 egg whites

2 tablespoons heavy whipping cream

TO BLEND

In a large mixing bowl, thoroughly blend seasonings and spices. Mix in ice-cold cubed meat and fat. Add garlic, egg whites and cream. Cover and refrigerate for 30 minutes. Fill another large mixing bowl with ice water; place all grinding equipment in bowl. (If the blade, plates or worm are not ice cold, they could heat up due to the friction during grinding. If this happens, the fat will melt and hinder the emulsification process.) After the equipment and meat have been chilled for 30 minutes, begin the grinding process.

TO GRIND

Fit grinder with a coarse grinding plate. Feed seasoned cubes of meat into the grinder. Place a mixing bowl resting in an ice-water bath under the grinding plates. Grind all meat into the chilled mixing bowl. Remove bowl from ice-water bath and replace with first bowl used to marinate the cubed meat; mix ground meat. Feed the ground meat through the grinder again to assure emulsification. Form one patty and cook in a small sauté pan over medium heat until cooked through; taste to check for seasoning and adjust if necessary. ▶

Rinse 36-38mm hog casings in clean running water. Slide casing over sink faucet and run water through casings. Fill cleaned casing with sausage, using a sausage stuffer or a pastry bag. Assure that casings are filled until firm, and limit amount of air gaps in casing by packing the stuffer tightly with the ground sausage. Once filled to desired length, tie casing with butcher's twine and start the process over again until all sausage is used. Hang finished sausage in refrigerator overnight so gravity can pack the sausage tighter.

TO COOK

Place sausage on a wire rack. Bake at 350° for 15-20 minutes or until internal temperature reaches 150°. Remove from the oven and spray with cool water to improve the appearance of the links. Cool at room temperature for 30 minutes. Cover and refrigerate or freeze until needed. ▪

Photo on page 75

PANCETTA
Makes 4 pounds

FROM THE CHEF ~ My pancetta is a variation on the classic rolled pancetta. I find the drying step works better for my applications. The drying time is faster, and the shape remains in a block for lardons.

4 ounces kosher salt

1 ounce brown sugar

1 ounce black pepper

½ ounce juniper berries, crushed

2 bay leaves, crushed

½ teaspoon ground nutmeg

½ tablespoon fresh thyme leaves

2 cloves garlic, thinly sliced

¼ ounce curing salt (sodium nitrite)

1 pork belly (5 pounds)

TO CURE

Combine the first nine ingredients and mix thoroughly; rub over the pork belly, making sure to cover all areas. Place in a plastic tub, skin side down. Cover and refrigerate for 10 days, overhauling (rubbing and rotating) every other day.

TO DRY

Rinse the pork with cool running water. Using a bacon hook, hang in the refrigerator to air-dry for 2-3 weeks. If you do not have room to hang the cured belly, place on a wire rack on a sheet pan on the top shelf of the refrigerator. Pancetta is ready once the belly is much firmer and no longer tacky to the touch. Trim sides of pancetta to form straight sides. Use trimmings in soups or sauces. Cover and refrigerate pancetta for up to 1 week, or vacuum-seal and freeze for up to 1 year. ▪

CIDER-POACHED FOIE GRAS TORCHON

Serves 12-15

1 Grade A foie gras   ¼ teaspoon curing salt   ½ gallon apple cider (preferably
    (1 to 1¼ pounds)   (sodium nitrite)   hard cider)
½ gallon milk   ½ teaspoon sugar
2 teaspoons kosher salt   ¼ teaspoon white pepper

FROM THE CHEF ~ "Torchon" comes from the French word for cloth, used to wrap the foie gras. This preparation of foie gras is the closest form of foie gras in the raw state. By using a ring to cut the torchon into a perfect circle, you are also cutting away the oxidized flesh. This oxidation is more about appearances than flavor.

TO SOAK

Place foie gras in a nonreactive container; cover with milk. Cover and refrigerate overnight. Remove from the milk and let stand at room temperature for 20 minutes to ease in the preparation.

TO CLEAN

Separate foie gras into its two lobes. With a paring knife, carefully scrape the thin transparent membrane surrounding the surface of the liver. Extricate the veins, with the bottom side up, by following the vein that starts at the narrow end and runs the length of the liver. Carefully dissect the lobe bilaterally with the tip of a paring knife. Using your fingers or fish tweezers, pull the vein from the lobe. There is another vein that runs parallel about ¼ inch below the first vein. Remember to remove any feather veins throughout the lobe. The more veins removed, the smoother the finished product. Repeat on other lobe. (See details and photos on page 194.)

TO SEASON AND CURE

Combine the salts, sugar and pepper; sprinkle evenly over foie gras. Sandwich the lobes together, putting the posterior and anterior ends together. Roll foie gras tightly in a 2-foot x 2-foot sheet of plastic wrap. Twist ends in opposite directions to tighten the cylinder even more. Refrigerate overnight. ▶

(fig. 1)

(fig. 2)

(fig. 3)

Let stand at room temperature for 20 minutes. Remove cured foie gras from plastic wrap; place at the end of a 2-foot square of cheesecloth.

Wrap cloth around cylinder and tuck into itself. (fig. 1)

Firmly press the edge of a sheet pan against foie gras while pulling the opposite end of cheesecloth. Roll cylinder in cheesecloth. (fig. 2)

Twist ends in opposite directions to tighten the cylinder even more. (fig. 3)

Tie ends tightly with butcher's twine.

(fig. 4)

(fig. 5)

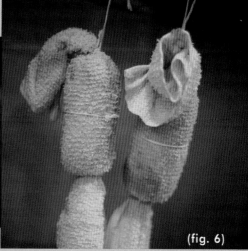

(fig. 6)

Submerge cloth-wrapped foie gras in simmering cider for 90 seconds. Immediately remove and shock in an ice-water bath. Cool for 20 minutes; remove from water and drain in a colander for 5 minutes. (fig. 4)

Wrap cheesecloth-lined foie gras in a clean dish towel, using the same method as with the cheesecloth. (fig. 5)

Tie ends tightly with butcher's twine.

Hang in the refrigerator overnight. (fig. 6)

Remove from the refrigerator and let stand at room temperature for 20 minutes. Remove cured foie gras from plastic wrap; place at the end of a 2-foot square of cheesecloth. Wrap cloth around cylinder and tuck into itself. Firmly press the edge of a sheet pan against foie gras while pulling the opposite end of cheesecloth. Roll cylinder in cheesecloth. Twist ends in opposite directions to tighten the cylinder even more; tie ends tightly with butcher's twine.

TO POACH AND PRESS

In a saucepan, bring cider to a gentle simmer. Submerge cloth-wrapped foie gras in cider for 90 seconds. Immediately remove and shock in an ice-water bath. Cool for 20 minutes; remove from water and drain in a colander for 5 minutes.

Wrap cheesecloth-lined foie gras in a clean dish towel. Using the same method as with the cheesecloth, tie the cylinder with butcher's twine and hang in the refrigerator overnight. Remove dish towel; unroll and discard cheesecloth. Tightly wrap the torchon in plastic wrap. Refrigerate for up to 1 week, or vacuum-seal and freeze for up to 1 year.

TO PLATE

With a hot wet knife, slice the foie gras into ½-inch to 1½-inch slices, using an even slicing motion. Use a metal ring to punch out the torchon slices into perfect circles. Serve with your favorite preparation or with toasted bread. ■

Photo on page 75

Satsuma Orange Jelly

Makes 2-3 pints

FROM THE CHEF ~ Satsuma oranges have
a distinct sweet flavor. If you can't find
satsumas, you may substitute fresh Mandarin
oranges or tangerines.

3½ cups satsuma orange juice, pulp removed
1½ teaspoons lemon juice
1 package powdered pectin
5 cups granulated sugar

In a high-sided nonreactive saucepan, bring juices
and pectin to a boil, stirring continuously. Boil for
1 minute (the boil should be a hard boil that will
not stir down). Add the sugar and bring to a hard
rolling boil for 1 minute. (This will allow for the
pectin and sugar to come to their full jelling abilities.)

Follow canning method on page 85. ▪

Prickly Pear Jelly

Makes 2-3 pints

FROM THE CHEF ~ Prickly pears are a fruit
that come from several kinds of cactus found
all over South and Central Texas. They have
many uses; however, this one works the best
with my charcuterie dishes. When I was a sous
chef, Creole Chef Jose Arevalo and Executive
Chef Carl Walker (now our General Manager)
would go hunting and bring back prickly pears
so I could make jelly. This goes great as a
glaze for quail or any other game.

1 quart ripe red prickly pears, rinsed
Water to cover
1 package powdered pectin
3 tablespoons lemon juice
3½ cups sugar

Wearing rubber gloves, peel the pears by cutting
off the ends and making an incision just through
the skin and down the length of the fruit. Peel the
skin back from the meat of the pear. Place fruit
in a large nonreactive saucepan; cover with water.
Bring to a boil and simmer until tender, about
15 minutes. Remove from the heat; strain through
double-lined cheesecloth or a clean pillowcase (do
not press fruit, or the juice will be cloudy and will
cloud the jelly). Drain overnight in the refrigerator
to extract as much juice as possible. You need
2½ cups for this recipe. ▶

In a high-sided nonreactive saucepan, bring prickly pear juice and pectin to a boil, stirring continuously. Boil for 1 minute (the boil should be a hard boil that will not stir down). Add the lemon juice and sugar; return to a hard rolling boil for 3 minutes. (This will allow for the pectin and sugar to come to their full jelling abilities.)

Follow canning method on page 85. ■

SATSUMA MARMALADE
Makes 4-5 pints

FROM THE CHEF ~ To make Meyer Lemon Marmalade, simply substitute 1½ pounds of Meyer lemons for the citrus in this recipe and prepare as directed.

1 pound satsuma oranges
½ pound lemons
4 cups water
4 cups sugar

Quarter each orange and lemon and remove the seeds with the tip of a paring knife. Tie the seeds in a cheesecloth bag; slice the lemons into ⅛-inch pieces. Place oranges, lemons and cheesecloth bag in a high-sided nonreactive saucepan; add water. Cover and let stand at room temperature overnight. (Soaking helps it become less bitter.)

Bring the orange and lemon mixture to a boil. Reduce heat and simmer until reduced to 4 cups, about 30 minutes. Stir in sugar. Boil over high heat, stirring often.

Follow canning method on page 85. ■

TEXAS PEACH PRESERVES
Makes 5 pints

FROM THE CHEF ~ Georgia may be famous for its peaches, but I think nothing compares to Texas peaches. One of my fondest childhood summertime memories is eating peaches from the roadside stand in Fairfield, Texas.

We would buy a 25-pound case and eat it during our visit ... on the way home, we'd buy two more cases — one for eating and the other for cooking. I am lucky enough to be able to use these same peaches from Cooper Farms from Memorial Day until Labor Day.

4½ pounds peaches, peeled,
   pitted and thinly sliced (4½ cups)
2 tablespoons lemon juice
1 package powdered pectin
7 cups sugar

Place the peaches, lemon juice and pectin in a high-sided nonreactive saucepan. Bring to a boil, stirring continuously. Boil for 1 minute (the boil should be a hard boil that will not stir down). Add the sugar and return to a hard rolling boil for 1 minute. (This will allow for the pectin and sugar to come to their full jelling abilities.) Skim the foam.

Follow canning method on page 85. ■

MAYHAW JELLY
Makes 2-3 pints

FROM THE CHEF ~ Mayhaw is a berry in the hawthorn family that has the aroma of overripe apples and pears with a tart finish. Once you add sugar, the tart flavor is balanced and makes a gorgeous red jelly. This jelly can be found up and down farm-to-market roads in east Texas and western Louisiana.

6 cups mayhaw berries, rinsed

4 cups water

5 cups granulated sugar

1 package powdered pectin

In a nonreactive saucepan, bring berries and water to a boil. Simmer for 15 minutes. Turn off heat; cover and let steep for 15 minutes. Strain through double-lined cheesecloth or a clean pillowcase (do not press fruit, or the juice will be cloudy and will cloud the jelly). Drain overnight in the refrigerator to extract as much juice as possible.

If juice measures less than 4¼ cups, add water to equal that amount. Place in a high-sided nonreactive saucepan. Add pectin. Bring to a boil, stirring continuously. Boil for 1 minute (the boil should be a hard boil that will not stir down). Add the sugar and bring to a hard rolling boil for 1 minute. (This will allow for the pectin and sugar to come to their full jelling abilities.)

Follow canning method on next page. ■

PRESERVING, CANNING or putting up of foodstuffs has been around since 1810, but it didn't come into vogue until the mid-1800s when the mason jar was invented. It has since fallen from the culinary world. Who needs to put up food when a plane can have fresh fruit and vegetables at your doorstep from the other side of the world in a day? I feel it's a lost art that our grandparents used to enjoy the flavors of the season year-round.

I spent a week at Texas A&M in the Food Science department, being certified in all methods of canning. There are multiple types of canning, but for our purposes, hot-water canning will suffice. Hot-water canning is useful when making jellies, jams, preserves and pickles. Remember to always practice proper sanitizing procedures spelled out in the instructions that come with the canning jars.

Below is the basic method for canning. Follow these instructions to can the jellies, marmalade and preserves on pages 81, 82 and 84.

TO CAN

Pour hot juice mixture into properly sanitized hot jars, leaving ¼-inch headspace (use a funnel to help keep the jelly off rim of jar). Wipe jar rims with a clean, damp cloth. Place sanitized lid on jar and then the band; screw band down finger-tight.

Process the jars in a boiling-water canner, making certain that the water is at least 1 inch above the jars, for 10 minutes. Remove from canner and place on a towel-lined surface; cool. Let stand overnight.

Check for proper seal by depressing on the lid. If lid pops, refrigerate and use as soon as possible. Label those that sealed properly and store in a cool, dark place.

VENISON AND SHINER BOCK SLIDERS

Serves 18

1 recipe Venison and Shiner Bock
    Sausage
1 recipe Silver Dollar Rolls or
    56 small sandwich buns
Softened butter
2 tablespoons mayonnaise
2 tablespoons Creole mustard
Jalapeño Bread-and-Butter Pickles
    (recipe on page 89)

VENISON AND
SHINER BOCK SAUSAGE*

2 pounds venison, cut into
    ½-inch cubes

2 pounds pork butt, cut into
    ½-inch cubes
1 pound pork fat, cut into
    ½-inch cubes
3 bottles (12 ounces *each*)
    Shiner Bock
3 tablespoons Creole Meat
    Seasoning (recipe on page 198)
2 tablespoons salt
½ teaspoon black pepper
¼ teaspoon granulated garlic
¼ teaspoon curing salt
    (sodium nitrite)
¼ teaspoon granulated onion

⅛ teaspoon mustard powder
⅛ teaspoon cayenne pepper
1 egg white
1 tablespoon heavy whipping cream

SILVER DOLLAR ROLLS

4 cups skim milk, *divided*
¼ cup dry yeast
5⅓ cups bread flour
¼ cup sugar
2 tablespoons salt
¼ cup shortening
6 eggs

FROM THE CHEF ~ I wanted a
sausage that represented Texas
Hill Country. The venison we use
is from Ingram, Texas, so it was
fitting to pair it with Shiner Bock,
a beer made in Shiner, Texas.

FOR THE SAUSAGE

Place cubed meat and fat in a large container; cover with
beer. Cover and refrigerate overnight. Drain and reserve
any beer that wasn't absorbed by the meat. Place beer in
a small saucepan; reduce over medium heat to ¼ cup.
Skim off any impurities. Cool for later use.

In a large mixing bowl, thoroughly blend seasonings and
spices. Mix in ice-cold cubed meat and fat. Add cold
reduced beer, egg white and cream. Cover and refrigerate
for 30 minutes. Fill another large mixing bowl with
ice water; place all grinding equipment in bowl. (If the
blade, plates or worm are not ice cold, they could heat
up due to the friction during grinding. If this happens,
the fat will melt and hinder the emulsification process.)
After the equipment and meat have been chilled for
30 minutes, begin grinding. ▶

Fit grinder with a coarse grinding plate. Feed seasoned cubes of meat into the grinder. Place a mixing bowl resting in an ice-water bath under the grinding plates. Grind all meat into the chilled mixing bowl. Remove bowl from ice-water bath and replace with first bowl used to marinate the cubed meat; mix ground meat. Feed the ground meat through the grinder again to assure emulsification.

Form one patty and cook in a small sauté pan over medium heat until cooked through; taste to check for seasoning and adjust if necessary. Form remaining sausage into 1½-ounce patties (#24 scoop). Refrigerate or freeze until needed.

FOR THE ROLLS

Warm 2 cups of milk to 105°-115° (be careful not to overheat, or it will kill the yeast). Sprinkle yeast over warm milk; allow 3-5 minutes to dissolve (bubbles will begin to form). Place flour, sugar and salt in the bowl of an electric mixer with a dough hook. Cut in shortening. Add 1 egg, then the yeast mixture. Mix on low speed until the dough begins to come together, then increase speed to medium. (This will help develop the glutens in the flour.)

Transfer the dough to a lightly oiled bowl; cover with a clean cloth. Place in a warm place (80°-82°) and allow to proof until the dough has doubled in size. Punch dough down and let rise again, about 15 minutes.

Portion the dough into 1-ounce pieces. Place dough, one piece at a time, between the palm of your slightly cupped hand and a lightly floured surface. Begin to swirl the dough in a clockwise motion to form into a ball. Place on a parchment-lined baking pan. For egg wash, beat the remaining eggs and milk; brush over dough. Proof in a warm place for 10-20 minutes. (Pan proofing or final proofing is best at a temperature of 90°-95° and humidity of 85%. This higher temperature and humidity produces a dough that has an even grain with good volume.) Bake at 400° for 15 minutes. Cool before using.

TO PLATE

On a greased griddle, sear sausage patties until cooked through, about 2 minutes on each side. Split rolls; butter the cut sides. Toast on a buttered griddle. Combine mayonnaise and mustard; spread over toasted rolls. Place patties on roll bottoms; top with pickles and roll tops. Serve three sliders per person. ■

If you want to stuff the sausage into casings instead of making patties, see the Lamb and Rosemary Sausage recipe, with directions for stuffing and cooking on page 77.

JALAPEÑO BREAD-AND-BUTTER PICKLES

Makes 4-5 pints

FROM THE CHEF ~ My favorite pickles are those with a little heat behind them. I make pickles out of jalapeños ... those are great with my Venison Sliders! I also add a few jalapeños to my regular bread-and-butter pickle recipe (see variation below) — the hot peppers pair well with the sweet-and-sour aspect of the pickles.

3 pounds jalapeño peppers

3 to 4 medium onions, thinly sliced

½ cup kosher salt

6 cups water

3 cups cider vinegar

2 cups packed brown sugar

2 tablespoons mustard seed

1 teaspoon celery seed

1 teaspoon ground cloves

¼ teaspoon turmeric

Wash jalapeños and remove the stem end. Cut into ¼-inch slices; place in a large bowl. Add onions, salt and water; mix well. Cover and let stand at room temperature for 2 hours. In a large saucepan, combine the vinegar, brown sugar, mustard seed, celery seed, cloves and turmeric. Bring to a boil. Drain jalapeños and onions; rinse off all residual salt and drain again. Add to vinegar mixture and return to a boil.

TO CAN

Pack hot pickles and liquid into properly sanitized hot jars, leaving ¼-inch headspace (use a funnel to help keep pickling liquid off rim of jar). Remove air bubbles with a straw or chopstick. Wipe jar rims with a clean, damp cloth. Place sanitized lid on jar and then the band; screw band down finger-tight.

Process the jars in a boiling-water canner, making certain that the water is at least 1 inch above the jars, for 10 minutes. Remove from canner and place on a towel-lined surface; cool. Let stand overnight. Check for proper seal by depressing on the lid. If lid pops, refrigerate and use as soon as possible. Label those that sealed properly and store in a cool, dark place.

BREAD-AND-BUTTER PICKLES

Prepare recipe as directed, substituting 3 pounds of pickling cucumbers and using just two jalapeños. Remove blossom end of each cucumber and cut into ¼-inch slices. Slice the jalapeños and combine with the cucumbers, onions, salt and water. ■

Note: It is very important to follow all sanitizing procedures spelled out in the packaging that comes with the canning jars.

SEAFOOD — SEAFOOD IS THE "MEAT AND POTATOES" of any

Creole kitchen. Don't sacrifice quality, because fresh fish will ensure a great outcome to your dish. Get to know your local fishmonger, and he'll steer you in the right direction. If a recipe calls for sturgeon, but the fishmonger says his salmon is better that day, be flexible and go with the salmon. Ask to smell the seafood before buying — it should smell like the ocean with a slight sweet finish. A reputable fishmonger should also know the place of origin ... location of harvest and farming can mean the difference in quality.

HALIBUT PROVENÇAL

GRILLED TUNA & TOMATOES

LOBSTER AMÉRICAINE

PEANUT-CRUSTED
SOFT-SHELL CRAB

PAN-SEARED RED SNAPPER

BLUE NOSE BASS
& CAULIFLOWER

CRAWFISH PIQUANT

JUMBO LUMP CRAB CAKES

TEXAS SHRIMP & BISCUITS

STURGEON &
BUTTERNUT HASH

HALIBUT PROVENÇAL
Serves 4

FROM THE CHEF ~ In mid-March, when Alaska's halibut season opens, my mouth begins to water. This is a great warm-weather dish. The fruity olive oil along with the brininess of the olives is refreshing on a hot day in Texas. By late spring, everything in this dish is in season — from the fish to the asparagus.

4 boneless skinless block-cut halibut fillets
  (6 ounces *each*)
Salt and white pepper to taste
3 tablespoons olive oil, *divided*
12 spears jumbo asparagus, blanched
1 recipe Yellow and Red Tomato Confit
1 recipe Olive Tapenade (see page 200)
1 recipe Chive Oil

YELLOW AND RED TOMATO CONFIT
4 yellow tomatoes, halved, peeled and seeded
4 Roma tomatoes, halved, peeled and seeded
¼ cup extra virgin olive oil
Kosher salt and cracked black pepper to taste
Red wine vinegar to taste

CHIVE OIL
½ cup minced chives
2 cups water
¼ cup salt
½ cup vegetable oil

FOR THE CONFIT
Toss the yellow and red tomatoes separately with oil, salt and pepper. Place on a parchment-lined baking sheet. Bake at 250° for 1½ hours or until partially dehydrated. Remove from the pan and refrigerate tomatoes in oil. Finely mince the tomatoes, keeping them separate. In separate small bowls, combine the tomatoes with a touch of vinegar and seasonings. Reserve for garnish.

FOR THE CHIVE OIL
Place chives in a fine mesh strainer. Bring water and salt to a boil; pour over chives over the sink. Dip strainer into an ice-water bath. Place chives in a blender with half of the oil; purée. Scrape down sides of blender. While processng, slowly add remaining oil. Transfer to a nonreactive container; refrigerate overnight. Strain oil through cheesecloth to remove chive particles. Reserve oil until needed.

FOR THE HALIBUT
Season fillets with salt and pepper. Heat 2 tablespoons olive oil in a large sauté pan over medium-high heat; sear halibut, belly side down, for 1 minute. Reduce heat to medium; cook 2 minutes longer. Do not turn over. Finish the halibut in a 450° oven for 4-5 minutes. Remove fillets from pan, flipping over with seared side facing up. Rest for 2 minutes.

TO PLATE
Sauté asparagus in remaining olive oil over medium-high heat for 3 minutes; season with salt and pepper. Arrange asparagus in center of plate with tips pointing out and ends meeting in the middle. Place a teaspoon of yellow tomato confit next to asparagus; place ½ tablespoon of tapenade next to the confit. Place a teaspoon of red tomato confit on other side of tapenade. Center halibut over asparagus. Drizzle chive oil around the plate. Serve immediately. ■

4 ripe tomatoes, sliced ½ inch thick

Micro greens

1 recipe Sugarcane Vinaigrette

SUGARCANE VINAIGRETTE

2½ tablespoons Steen's sugarcane vinegar

1 tablespoon Steen's sugarcane syrup

1 tablespoon vegetable oil

Salt and black pepper to taste

FOR THE VINAIGRETTE

In a small mixing bowl, combine vinegar and syrup. Whisk in oil. Season to taste. Can be stored in the refrigerator for up to 1 month.

FOR THE TUNA

Heat grill on high heat. Season tuna with salt and pepper; rub both sides with oil. Place on grill for 1 minute. Turn tuna a quarter turn and grill 1 minute longer. Grill other side of tuna in the same manner. I recommend serving the tuna rare to medium-rare, but if you prefer it well-done, cook longer.

TO PLATE

Season the tomato slices and place flat on the plate. Top with tuna and micro greens. Drizzle vinaigrette over tuna and tomatoes and around the plate. Serve immediately. ■

GRILLED TUNA WITH
HOMEGROWN TOMATOES
Serves 4

FROM THE CHEF ~ Tomatoes should only be served at their peak of ripeness to enjoy their full flavor. The same goes for tuna — it should only be eaten at its peak of freshness.

4 center-cut yellowfin tuna steaks (2 to 3 inches thick and 6 ounces *each*)

Salt and black pepper to taste

2 tablespoons vegetable oil

LOBSTER AMÉRICAINE

Serves 4

4 lobsters (1 ½ to 2 pounds each)

1 recipe Court-Bouillon

1 recipe Sauce Américaine

1 egg yolk

1 tablespoon cold water

2 sheets puff pastry

2 tablespoons water

1 pound unsalted butter, cubed

24 spears fresh asparagus (2 inches long), blanched

Salt and black pepper to taste

1 recipe Celeriac-Apple Salad

COURT-BOUILLON

¼ cup vegetable oil

½ cup coarsely chopped onion

¼ cup coarsely chopped carrot

¼ cup coarsely chopped celery

1 clove garlic, smashed

1 lemon, halved

2 tablespoons dry white wine

1 tablespoon salt

1 teaspoon black peppercorns

2 quarts water

SAUCE AMÉRICAINE

¼ cup vegetable oil

½ cup coarsely chopped onion

¼ cup coarsely chopped carrot

¼ cup coarsely chopped celery

FROM THE CHEF ~ We roll out this showstopper every New Year's Eve. I suggest treating all lobsters in this fashion — by cooking the lobster in its segments, you can control the cook time of the different thicknesses. This method yields sweet, tender tail meat without overcooking the thinner claw and knuckle meat.

Break apart the live lobsters by first twisting off the tail from the thorax. Remove claws and knuckles from rest of the body. Separate top of the head from the bottom half of the thorax. Remove the coral (innards) from the body cavity. Slide a bamboo skewer through the tail to keep the tails from curling while poaching. Reserve lobster segments.

FOR THE COURT-BOUILLON

Heat oil in a stockpot over medium heat; sweat the onion, carrot and celery for 3-4 minutes. Add garlic, lemon, wine, salt, peppercorns and water. Bring to a boil. Fill a large bowl with ice water. Submerge the skewered shell-on lobster tails in the simmering water; poach for 4 minutes. Remove the tails and shock in the ice bath. ▶

3¾ teaspoons tomato paste

1 teaspoon black peppercorns

1 clove garlic, smashed

1 small bay leaf

½ sprig thyme

Reserved lobster shells

6¾ teaspoons brandy, *divided*

2 tablespoons dry white wine

½ cup all-purpose flour

1 cup heavy whipping cream

Salt and white pepper to taste

¾ teaspoon dry vermouth

CELERIAC-APPLE SALAD

¼ cup julienned peeled celeriac

½ Granny Smith apple, julienned

1 tablespoon shaved celery

1 teaspoon brunoise jalapeño,
    seeds removed

½ ounce micro celery

2 teaspoons olive oil

Juice of 1 lime

Salt and black pepper to taste

Poach lobster claws and knuckles in the simmering water for 2 minutes; shock in ice bath. Once lobster has cooled, remove from ice bath. Remove meat from shells, using kitchen shears. Reserve the meat. With the shears, trim head to 3 inches long and tail fins to 2 inches long. The remaining shells will be used for the sauce. Reserve poaching liquid.

FOR THE SAUCE

Heat oil in a stockpot over medium heat; sweat the onion, carrot and celery until vegetables lose some of their liquid and onion starts to become translucent. Mix in tomato paste and caramelize over high heat. Add peppercorns, garlic, bay leaf, thyme and reserved crushed lobster shells; sauté for 5 minutes.

Deglaze pan with 2 tablespoons brandy and wine. With a wooden spoon, scrape bottom of pan to release the fond; cook for 5 minutes over medium heat, until almost dry. Stir in flour; cook for 10 minutes, stirring often to keep flour from burning. Add reserved poaching liquid; bring to a simmer. Simmer for 10 minutes on low heat. Pour in cream and return to a low simmer; continue to cook for 30 minutes to cook out the flour taste. Adjust seasonings. Add vermouth and remaining brandy to help add a crisp acidity to the sauce.

Strain sauce through a strainer, pushing down on the lobster and vegetable mixture to extract all the flavor and liquid. Strain again through a fine mesh strainer to refine the sauce. Keep warm until serving. Sauce can be refrigerated for up to 2 days.

FOR THE PUFF PASTRY VOL-AU-VENT

In a small bowl, beat egg yolk and cold water. Cut cold puff pastry into eight 3-inch x 4-inch rectangles. Working quickly, cut a 2-inch x 3-inch rectangle from the center of four rectangles. Brush solid puff pastry with egg wash; top with trimmed rectangles. Brush edges with egg wash. Place on a baking sheet. Bake at 375° for 12 minutes or until golden.

FOR THE SALAD

In a small mixing bowl, combine all ingredients at the last minute. This will add a nice textural contrast to the dish.

TO PLATE

In a medium saucepan over medium-high heat, bring 2 tablespoons water to a simmer; whisk in cold butter, cube by cube. Season lobster meat with salt and pepper; add skewered tail meat and claws to the hot butter. Heat through on low for 15 minutes. Add asparagus; warm for 3-4 minutes.

On each plate, place six asparagus spears, with tips facing out three to the left and three to the right. Lay warm pastry over asparagus, with tips of rectangle running perpendicular to asparagus. Arrange the hot lobster claws next to each other in front of asparagus. Place the head facing away from the pastry. Remove skewers from the tail and lay opposite the head with the tail fin following. (The plate should resemble a lobster.) Toss the salad with the lobster knuckle meat; spoon over tail. Drizzle sauce around the plate and serve immediately. ∎

PEANUT-CRUSTED SOFT-SHELL CRAB
Serves 4

1 recipe Lemongrass Vinaigrette

1 medium sweet onion, shaved

¼ cup Tabasco

1½ cups all-purpose flour

2½ teaspoons Creole Seafood
   Seasoning (recipe on page 198),
   divided

Oil for frying

1 pound jumbo lump crabmeat,
   picked over for shells, *divided*

1 pint sweet grape tomatoes,
   oven-roasted

6 cups arugula, cleaned and
   stems removed

1 recipe Spiced Peanuts
   (recipe on page 199)

½ cup dried breadcrumbs

2 tablespoons Ravigote Sauce
   (recipe on page 198)

4 large soft-shell crabs, cleaned

1 egg

½ cup milk

LEMONGRASS VINAIGRETTE

1 stalk lemongrass, roughly chopped

½ cup vegetable oil

Juice and zest of 1 lemon

2 tablespoons rice wine vinegar

1 tablespoon chili garlic sauce

1 teaspoon minced garlic

1 teaspoon Dijon mustard

1 teaspoon Sriracha Hot Chili Sauce

1 teaspoon salt

1 teaspoon sugar

FROM THE CHEF ~ The secret to having the best and meatiest soft-shell crabs is the stuffing. Guests are always commenting on how much crabmeat our soft-shells have ... the secret is we add jumbo lump crabmeat to them.

Once you've had a fresh, live soft-shell crusted and fried, you'll agree all the effort was worth it.

FOR THE VINAIGRETTE

Wrap lemongrass in cheesecloth and place in a small saucepan; add oil. Bring to a simmer; remove from the heat and steep for 1 hour. In a mixing bowl, combine remaining ingredients. Slowly whisk in the lemongrass oil. Adjust seasoning as needed.

FOR THE SALAD

In a bowl, marinate shaved onion in Tabasco for 30 minutes. Season flour with 1½ teaspoons seafood seasoning; toss 1 cup seasoned flour with onions. In a deep fryer, heat oil to 375°; fry onions. In a large mixing bowl, gently toss ½ pound lump crabmeat, tomatoes, arugula, ¼ cup Lemongrass Vinaigrette and fried onions.

FOR THE CRAB

Set aside ¼ cup peanuts. Pulse the remaining peanuts in a food processor until fine but not oily. Blend in breadcrumbs; set aside. Combine the remaining ►

lump crabmeat with Ravigote Sauce and remaining seafood seasoning; stuff into the soft-shell crabs. Dust crabs with remaining seasoned flour. In a small bowl, beat egg and milk; dip crabs into egg wash. Coat with reserved peanut mixture. In a deep fryer, heat oil to 375°; fry crabs for

3-5 minutes or until golden. Drain on a wire rack.

TO PLATE

Place salad in the center of the plate; top with the fried soft-shell. Finish with a drizzle of vinaigrette around the plate. Serve while crab is still crispy. ■

PAN-SEARED AMERICAN RED SNAPPER

Serves 6

6 American red snapper fillets
   (6 ounces *each*), skin on
   and scales removed
¼ cup vegetable oil
Salt and white pepper to taste

MORNAY SAUCE

¼ cup unsalted butter
2 tablespoons minced garlic

¼ cup sliced shallots
1 cup sliced leeks (white portion only)
1 teaspoon salt
⅛ teaspoon black pepper
¼ cup all-purpose flour
2¼ cups milk
2 tablespoons white wine
½ tablespoon choppped fresh herbs
1 cup shredded Gruyère

GOLD BAR SQUASH GRATIN

2 large tomatoes, cut into
   ⅛-inch slices
4½ tablespoons olive oil, *divided*
½ tablespoon minced garlic
Salt and black pepper to taste
4 pounds gold bar squash, cut
   lengthwise into ¼-inch slices
¾ cup dry breadcrumbs

FROM THE CHEF ~

Red snapper is prized for its sweet flesh and light flake like the redfish of the blackened redfish craze in the 1980s. I use only American red snapper. To secure the future of this fish in our native waters, the U.S. Government has a season for commercial fishing of red snapper. It is our job as chefs and consumers to sustain these wild species for future generations.

FOR THE MORNAY SAUCE

Melt butter in a saucepan over medium heat; sweat garlic, shallots, leeks, salt and pepper until vegetables are translucent, about 3-4 minutes. Add flour; cook for 3 minutes to cook out the starch. Whisk in milk; bring to a simmer. Simmer for 30 minutes. Whisk in wine and herbs. Remove from the heat; stir in cheese until thoroughly combined.

FOR THE GRATIN

Rub tomato slices with 2 tablespoons olive oil; season with garlic, salt and pepper. Place on a wire rack on a baking sheet. Bake at 300° until dry, but not brown. Season squash slices with salt and pepper. Place on a wire rack on a baking sheet. Bake at 300° for 30-45 minutes. In a food processor, pulse breadcrumbs, grated cheese, herbs, ¼ teaspoon salt and ⅛ teaspoon pepper. Slowly add remaining olive oil. ▶

¼ cup grated Gruyère

½ tablespoon chopped fresh herbs

¼ teaspoon salt

⅛ teaspoon black pepper

⅓ cup shredded Gruyère

¾ cup fresh spinach, blanched
   and squeezed dry

1 recipe Mornay Sauce

CRABMEAT-TARRAGON SAUCE

½ cup cold unsalted butter, *divided*

2 tablespoons minced shallot

½ pound jumbo lump crabmeat,
   picked over for shells

½ tablespoon chopped fresh
   tarragon

¼ cup dry vermouth

Grease a loaf pan; line with a third of the squash, 2 tablespoons shredded cheese, ¼ cup spinach, 3 ounces Mornay sauce and a third of the tomatoes. Repeat layers twice. Top with remaining sauce; sprinkle with seasoned breadcrumbs. Cover with foil. Bake at 350° for 25-30 minutes, removing foil for the last 10 minutes to toast the crumbs. Let rest for 10 minutes before serving.

FOR THE SNAPPER

With the edge of a knife, scrape skin of snapper to remove any excess water (like using a squeegee). Score the skin by just cutting through it. Season fillets with salt and pepper.

Heat vegetable oil in a large sauté pan over high heat; sear snapper, skin side down, for 1 minute. Reduce heat to medium; cook 2 minutes longer. Do not turn over. Finish the snapper in a 450°

oven for 3-4 minutes. Remove fillets from pan, flipping over with skin side up. Rest for 2 minutes.

FOR THE CRABMEAT SAUCE

Melt 2 tablespoons butter in a medium sauté pan over medium heat; sweat shallot for 3 minutes or until translucent. Add crabmeat, tarragon and vermouth. Increase heat and bring to a simmer; reduce vermouth until almost dry. Remove from the heat; swirl in remaining cold butter, using the back of a spoon to incorporate. Work quickly and gently to emulsify sauce and to keep from breaking up the lumps of crab.

TO PLATE

Cut gratin into six even slices; place in center of plate. Top with snapper fillet, crispy skin side up. Spoon crabmeat sauce around the plate. Serve hot. ■

BLUE NOSE BASS WITH CAULIFLOWER PURÉE

Serves 4

FROM THE CHEF ~ Blue Nose Bass is a great variety of fish from the waters surrounding New Zealand. It has a shellfish-like flavor and meaty texture. By cooking the cauliflower in milk, we are able to get rid of the earthy flavor that many people dislike about cauliflower and bring out its natural sweetness.

4 tablespoons vegetable oil, *divided*

4 Blue Nose Bass fillets (6 ounces *each*), skin on and scales removed

Salt and white pepper to taste

4 dry-packed diver sea scallops (U-10 or larger)

1 recipe Cauliflower Purée

1 recipe Wild Mushroom Ragoût (see page 200)

CAULIFLOWER PURÉE

1 head cauliflower, sliced into florets

1 quart whole milk

Salt and white pepper to taste

2 tablespoons vegetable oil

FOR THE CAULIFLOWER

In a saucepan, combine cauliflower, milk, salt and pepper. Bring to a simmer; cook for 30 minutes or until cauliflower is very soft. Strain any residual milk through a colander, reserving milk for later use. Purée cauliflower in a blender; add enough of the reserved milk until cauliflower is smooth (should be the consistency of loose mashed potatoes). While blender is still running,

incorporate oil to help add a satiny finish. Adjust seasoning as needed. Keep warm.

FOR THE BASS AND SCALLOPS

Heat 2 tablespoons oil in a large sauté pan over high heat; sear bass, skin side down, for 1 minute. Reduce heat to medium; cook 2 minutes longer. Do not turn over. Finish the bass in a 450° oven for 5-6 minutes or until firm to the touch.

Meanwhile, heat remaining oil in a small sauté pan; season scallops and sear for 2 minutes on each side. (Do not overcook; scallops should be slightly gray in the center.) Remove fillets from oven and remove from pan, flipping over with skin side up. Rest for 2 minutes.

TO PLATE

Spoon the cauliflower purée in the center of the plate; place bass, skin side up, over purée. Slice scallops in half horizontally; arrange fanned out, resting on the bass. Spoon mushroom ragoût around purée and serve immediately. ∎

When pulled from the water, all tuna is considered sashimi grade ... the time out of the water and the handling can change its quality. The art of grading tuna can take years. A test plug is taken behind the gill and a cross section taken from the tail to show color and texture throughout the entire fish. All tuna is graded based on these two test areas.

It's interesting to watch the haggling between the captain of the boat and the fishmonger purchasing the fish. The captain always wants #1++ fish, while the monger would like to negotiate, saying the fish is only a #1+. This small variance can mean several dollars a pound on the retail side.

This grading scale can inform the chef/consumer of the freshness of the fish and how well the fish was handled while out of the water. These grade differences are hardly discernible to the untrained eye, but in the tuna markets of Japan and Hawaii, they make a world of difference. Some #1++ bluefin tuna go for thousands of dollars at auction.

Grading Scale

#1 ++
#1 +
#1   = sashimi grade
#2 ++
#2 +
#2
Grill grade

CRAWFISH SAUCE PIQUANT

Serves 8

FROM THE CHEF ~ Fresh Louisiana crawfish tails are the secret to any good crawfish dish. Crawfish season is from late winter to early summer. Support our Louisiana crawfish farmer!

2 tablespoons vegetable oil

2 pounds crawfish tail meat

3 tablespoons Creole Seafood Seasoning
   (recipe on page 198)

1 recipe Sauce Base

2½ tablespoons chopped fresh herbs (thyme,
   basil and oregano)

1 recipe Louisiana Popcorn Rice

¼ cups chopped green onions

(recipe on page 198)

SAUCE BASE

1 cup vegetable oil

2 cups all-purpose flour, *divided*

2 cups medium diced yellow onion

½ cup medium diced green bell pepper

½ cup medium diced red bell pepper

4 jalapeños, seeded and diced

1 cup medium diced celery

3 tablespoons minced garlic

2 tablespoons Creole Seafood Seasoning
   (recipe on page 198)

1½ teaspoons red pepper flakes

½ cup Worcestershire sauce

1 tablespoon Louisiana hot sauce

4 medium tomatoes, peeled, seeded, cored and diced

½ cup red wine

1 quart Veal Stock (recipe on page 201)
   or low-sodium beef broth

1 cup water

2 bay leaves

LOUISIANA POPCORN RICE

2 tablespoons unsalted butter

2 tablespoons vegetable oil

1 mirliton, peeled, seeded and diced

¼ cup diced yellow onion

1 cup popcorn rice (see Source Guide on
   page 204) or other aromatic rice

2 cups Chicken Stock (recipe on page 201)
   or low-sodium chicken broth

Salt and black pepper to taste

2 tablespoons grated Parmesan cheese

2 tablespoons finely sliced chives

FOR THE SAUCE

Heat oil in a large cast-iron or stainless pot over high heat for 5-6 minutes or until the oil just starts to smoke. Gently add a third of the flour, stirring constantly with a long wooden spoon. Cook for 30 seconds, stirring constantly, until flour begins to brown. Add another third of flour and stir constantly for 30 seconds or until well incorporated. Add remaining flour; cook and stir for 2-3 minutes. The roux should be a dark shade of brown.

Add the onion, bell peppers, jalapeños, celery and garlic, being extremely cautious of the steam released from the vegetables. Cook over medium-low heat until vegetables are wilted, about 3-5 minutes. Add seafood seasoning, pepper flakes, Worcestershire sauce and hot sauce; cook, stirring constantly, for 2 minutes. Add tomatoes and wine; cook for 3 minutes. Add the stock, water and bay leaves; bring to a boil. Reduce heat and simmer for 30 minutes. Keep warm. ▶

Melt butter with oil in a saucepan over high heat; sauté mirliton until slightly caramelized, about 3 minutes. Reduce heat to medium; sweat onion for 3 minutes or until translucent. Add rice; cook, stirring constantly, for 4 minutes or until a toasty aroma develops. Add broth, salt and pepper.

Bring to a boil and reduce to a simmer. Cover and cook over low heat for 10-12 minutes or until all of the liquid is absorbed. (Or cover and bake at 350° for 30 minutes.) Using a fork, separate the grains of rice. Stir in Parmesan cheese and chives. Adjust seasoning as needed. Keep warm.

Heat oil in a large saucepan over high heat. Add the crawfish and seafood seasoning; cook for 2 minutes. Add sauce base and herbs. Bring to a simmer. Place a scoop of popcorn rice in the center of a warm bowl; ladle the crawfish sauce around the rice. Garnish with a sprinkling of green onions. ▪

JUMBO LUMP CRAB CAKES
Serves 5 (for entrée) or 10 (for appetizer)

FROM THE CHEF ~ People from the Texas Coast take their Blue Crab cakes as seriously as residents of Maryland do. When corn is at its sweetest, so are the Blue Crabs in the Gulf of Mexico.

1 cup roasted corn (about 2 ears)

2 tablespoons fire-roasted red bell peppers, skinned, seeded and diced

1 cup mayonnaise

2 tablespoons chopped parsley

½ tablespoon Creole Seafood Seasoning (recipe on page 198)

Juice of ½ lime

Salt and pepper to taste

2 pounds jumbo lump crabmeat, picked over for shells

1 tablespoon oil

1 recipe Sweet Corn Leek Sauce

1 recipe Mirliton Slaw

SWEET CORN LEEK SAUCE

4 ears yellow corn

1 tablespoon vegetable oil

1 leek (white portion only), chopped

¼ cup finely diced sweet onion

2 cups water

1 cup heavy whipping cream

Juice of ½ lime

¾ teaspoon kosher salt

¼ teaspoon white pepper

MIRLITON SLAW

1 tablespoon vegetable oil

2 teaspoons Steen's sugarcane vinegar

1 teaspoon Steen's sugarcane syrup

1 small carrot, peeled and julienned

1 small mirliton (chayote), peeled and julienned

2 leaves radicchio, chiffonade

¼ cup sweet pea shoots

Salt and pepper to taste

FOR THE CRAB CAKES

In a bowl combine the corn, peppers, mayonnaise, parsley, seafood seasoning, lime juice, salt and pepper; add crab and fold together, taking care to not break up the crabmeat. Pack the mixture into 2½-inch metal cookie cutter rings. Heat oil in a large cast-iron pan or griddle over medium heat. Place rings in the pan. Cook crab cakes for 3 minutes on each side until golden brown.

FOR THE SAUCE

Remove kernels from cobs. Scrape the cobs with the back of a knife and add milk to the kernels. Set cobs aside. Heat oil in a saucepan over medium-high heat; sauté the corn, leek and onion for 5 minutes or until translucent. Add reserved cobs and cover with water. Bring to a boil; reduce heat. Simmer for 30 minutes. Add cream; cook 10 minutes longer. Remove and discard cobs. Add lime juice, salt and pepper. Purée sauce in a blender and strain through a fine mesh strainer.

FOR THE SLAW

In a bowl, combine the oil, vinegar and syrup. Add remaining ingredients; toss and season to taste.

TO PLATE

Ladle sauce to cover plate; center crab cakes and gently slide off rings. Top with slaw. ■

seafood

Wild Texas Shrimp with "Biscuits and Gravy"

Serves 6

FROM THE CHEF ~ This dish was conceived as a last-minute recipe for the 2005 Great American Seafood Cook-Off. Texas Governor Rick Perry named me as the Texas chef to compete against chefs from other seafood-producing states. As luck would have it, I was named "King of Seafood."

½ cup Honey-Cured Bacon lardons (recipe on page 71)
2 tablespoons vegetable oil
30 white Texas shrimp (9-12 count with heads on)
Kosher salt to taste
Cayenne pepper to taste
2 tablespoons white wine
¼ cup Texas honey
2 tablespoons cold unsalted butter, *divided*
1 recipe Shrimp Gravy
1 recipe Buttermilk Biscuit Pudding
¼ cup bias-cut green onions

BUTTERMILK BISCUITS

1 cup all-purpose flour
½ tablespoon baking powder
¼ teaspoon baking soda
¼ teaspoon salt
2 tablespoons cold shortening
½ cup cold buttermilk

BUTTERMILK BISCUIT PUDDING

1 tablespoon unsalted butter
1½ cups julienned sweet onion
½ cup sliced leeks (white portion only)
¼ cup sliced shallots
2 cloves garlic, shaved
¼ cup minced celery
1 recipe Buttermilk Biscuits
½ tablespoon chopped fresh thyme
¼ cup sliced green onions
2 eggs
1 cup heavy whipping cream
Salt and black pepper to taste

SHRIMP GRAVY

1 tablespoon unsalted butter
1 shallot, roughly chopped
½ tablespoon tomato paste
¼ cup brandy
¼ cup vermouth
1 teaspoon black peppercorns
1 bay leaf
1 sprig thyme
2 cups Shrimp Stock (recipe on page 202)
1 cup heavy whipping cream

FOR THE BISCUITS

In a small mixing bowl, combine the dry ingredients. Cut in the shortening. Add buttermilk and mix just until combined. Roll out on a floured surface ½ inch thick. Cut out 6 biscuits. Place on a baking sheet. Bake at 325° for 20 minutes.

FOR THE PUDDING

Melt butter in a medium sauté pan on medium-low heat. Add the onion, leeks, shallots and garlic; cook until caramelized. Add celery and cook until tender. Crumble the baked biscuits into a mixing bowl; fold in the onion mixture, thyme and green onions. In a separate bowl, whisk the eggs ▶

and cream. Pour over biscuit mixture and fold together. Season with salt and pepper. Spoon into greased 2½-inch steel rings or biscuit cutters. Bake at 300° for 20-25 minutes. Keep warm.

FOR THE GRAVY

Melt 1 tablespoon butter in a small saucepan over medium-low heat; sweat shallot until translucent. Add tomato paste and cook until caramelized. Deglaze pan with brandy and vermouth. Add peppercorns, bay leaf and thyme. Reduce until almost dry. Add stock and cream; bring to a boil. Reduce heat to low; simmer for 1 hour or until the sauce almost coats the back of a spoon. Strain through a fine mesh strainer. Keep warm.

FOR THE SHRIMP

Heat a small sauté pan over medium-high heat; render bacon lardons until crispy. Set aside. Heat oil in a large sauté pan over medium-high heat. Peel and devein shrimp, being careful not to loosen the heads or tails, season with salt; sauté in oil. Sprinkle with cayenne. Once the shrimp are almost cooked, but still slightly gray in the center, deglaze pan with wine and honey. Allow shrimp to cook through; remove from pan and keep warm. Emulsify 1 tablespoon cold butter into the honey glaze.

TO PLATE

Bring shrimp gravy to a boil; remove from heat. Add remaining cold butter and emulsify with a handheld blender. Place biscuit pudding in center of plate. Surround with a pool of gravy and arrange shrimp around the pudding. Drizzle with honey glaze; sprinkle with green onions and bacon lardons. ■

COLUMBIA RIVER STURGEON WITH BUTTERNUT HASH
Serves 4

FROM THE CHEF ~ Thick, meaty fish like sturgeon can benefit from low-heat poaching, which ensures the entire fish remains moist while cooking.

1 recipe Butternut Squash Hash

2 cups olive oil

4 boneless skinless block-cut sturgeon fillets
   (6 ounces *each*)

Salt and white pepper to taste

1 recipe Sage Butter Sauce

BUTTERNUT SQUASH HASH

1½ cups cubed peeled butternut squash
   (½-inch cubes)

4 teaspoons oil, *divided*

Salt and white pepper to taste

3 tablespoons pancetta lardons (¼-inch cubes)

1 leek (white portion only), thinly shaved

1 clove garlic, thinly shaved

1 teaspoon minced chives

SAGE BUTTER SAUCE

½ cup unsalted butter, cubed

2 teaspoons chopped fresh sage

Juice of ½ lemon

Salt and white pepper to taste

FOR THE HASH

Toss squash with 3 teaspoons oil, salt and pepper. Place on a baking sheet. Bake at 350° for 40 minutes or until tender and slightly browned. Meanwhile, in a sauté pan, heat remaining oil over medium heat; render pancetta until crispy. Use a slotted spoon to remove to a small container. In the fat, sauté leek and garlic over medium-high heat for 2 minutes or until garlic begins to brown slightly. Add warm squash and pancetta. Adjust seasoning. Add chives; toss. Keep warm.

FOR THE STURGEON

In a straight-sided sauté pan, heat olive oil slowly to 120°. Season the fillets and carefully submerge in hot oil. Cook over low heat, maintaining the temperature, for 20 minutes. Sturgeon is ready when firm but still slightly gray inside.

FOR THE SAUCE

Melt butter in a small sauté pan over medium-high. Once melted, increase the heat and allow butter to begin to brown. Remove from the heat; stir in the sage, lemon juice, salt and pepper.

TO PLATE

Arrange butternut hash in the center of the plate; top with poached sturgeon. Pour a little of the sauce over the fish and around the plate. ∎

M EAT — THIS CHAPTER DEFINES

"TEXAS" in our Texas-Creole menu philosophy. I like

to highlight that fact that Texas is a wild game hunting

state by including selections from venison to game birds.

Our side dishes are influenced by the immigrants who

settled here. For example, I give a Louisiana twist to

German spaetzle by making it with sweet potatoes ...

and I add jalapeños to the cornbread custard served

with the lamb.

What we try to accomplish at the Kitchen Table is to

take familiar items and make them completely new —

like giving beef tenderloin a crust featuring cocoa nibs,

or serving a Wellington "inside out" with veal medallions

and a mushroom ragoût on top of puff pastry. The

recipes that follow are a selection of our favorites.

LAMB WITH
CORNBREAD CUSTARD

SIKA VENISON &
JOHNNYCAKES

VEAL "WELLINGTON"

TRUFFLE-SCENTED POUSSIN

DUCK POT PIE

TEXAS BOBWHITE QUAIL

BLACK LACQUERED DUCK

RABBIT THREE WAYS

PORK & SPAETZLE

SOCO SHORT RIBS

COCOA NIB CHÂTEAUBRIAND

LAMB WITH MUSTARD GREENS AND CORNBREAD CUSTARD

Serves 8

FROM THE CHEF ~ We use grain-fed lamb from Colorado. The meat has a sweet finish, not the "mutton" flavor that many people dislike. My idea for the mustard greens started with a savory mustard green soufflé. I'd made the base for the soufflé, and our wine guy ate an entire bowl of it! He said I should stop there, so I did, feeling I couldn't improve on it any further.

24 lamb chops, frenched

¼ cup Creole Meat Seasoning (recipe on page 198)

3 tablespoons vegetable oil

1½ pounds Lamb and Rosemary Sausage (recipe on page 76), bias-cut into 8 slices

1 recipe Creamed Mustard Greens

1 recipe Cornbread Custard

1 recipe Jack Daniels Creole Mustard Demi-Glace

CREAMED MUSTARD GREENS

3 bunches mustard greens

2 tablespoons vegetable oil, *divided*

1 yellow onion, finely diced

1 tablespoon minced garlic

½ cup diced tasso ham

¾ cup Chicken Stock (recipe on page 201) or low-sodium chicken broth

1 tablespoon all-purpose flour

1 cup milk

2 teaspoons cider vinegar

2 teaspoons salt

1 teaspoon pepper

Tabasco to taste

CORNBREAD CUSTARD

1 tablespoon vegetable oil

1½ cups fresh corn kernels (about 3 ears)

½ cup chopped yellow onion

4 eggs

2 cups heavy whipping cream

4½ cups crumbled Cornbread (recipe on page 203)

1½ cups shredded jalapeño Jack cheese, *divided*

Salt and white pepper to taste

JACK DANIELS CREOLE MUSTARD DEMI-GLACE

1 teaspoon butter

1 shallot, roughly chopped

¼ cup Creole mustard

½ cup Jack Daniels

1¼ cups Veal Demi-Glace (recipe on page 201)

Salt to taste

FOR THE GREENS

Wash mustard greens thoroughly three times; tear into pieces. Heat 1 tablespoon oil in a large sauté pan; sauté onion and ham for 2 minutes. Add garlic; sweat until aromatic. Add the greens; cover and cook for 5 minutes. Add stock; simmer, uncovered, until greens are tender, about 30 minutes.

Make a roux with flour and remaining oil. Add milk to the greens; bring to a boil. Slowly stir in roux; simmer for 30 minutes. Finish with vinegar, salt, pepper and Tabasco. ▶

Heat oil in a medium sauté pan over medium-high heat; sauté corn and onion until onion is translucent. In a large bowl, whisk eggs and cream. Blend in corn mixture, cornbread crumbs and 1 cup cheese. Add salt and pepper. Pour into a greased 8-inch square baking pan. Sprinkle with remaining cheese.

Cover pan with plastic wrap and aluminum foil; place in a larger baking pan. Fill larger pan with hot water to within ½ inch of top of square pan. Bake at 325° for 1½ hours or until custard is firm in center. Let stand for 5 minutes before serving.

FOR THE DEMI-GLACE

Melt butter in a small saucepan over medium heat; sweat shallot for 3 minutes or until translucent. Add mustard and Jack Daniels. Increase heat and reduce by two-thirds. Add demi-glace; simmer for 5 minutes or until mixture reaches sauce consistency. Adjust seasoning. Keep warm, or refrigerate for 1 week or freeze up to 6 months.

FOR THE LAMB

Season the lamb with Creole seasoning; rub with oil. Wrap bones in foil. Grill the lamb and sausage slices over hot heat for 2 minutes; turn 90° to create cross marks and grill 2 minutes longer. Repeat for the other side. Let rest for 5 minutes.

TO PLATE

Spoon greens onto center of plate; top with a square of custard. Lean three lamb chops against the custard. Position the lamb sausage against the bones; drizzle demi-glace on and around lamb. ■

Photo on page 112

SIKA VENISON WITH TEXAS FIELD PEA FRICASSEE

Serves 4

1 back-strap venison loin
   (1½ pounds)
Creole Meat Seasoning to taste
   (recipe on page 198)
4 tablespooons vegetable oil, *divided*
8 Bacon and Corn Johnnycakes
1 recipe Texas Field Pea Fricassee

BACON-CORN JOHNNYCAKES

½ cup all-purpose flour, sifted
¼ cup corn flour (masa)
¼ cup cornmeal
1 teaspoon baking powder

1 tablespoon granulated sugar
1 teaspoon salt
½ cup milk
1 egg, *separated*
2 tablespoons butter, melted
4 ounces Honey-Cured Bacon
   Lardons (⅛-inch cubes)
   (recipe on page 71)
1 ear sweet corn, shucked and
   kernels cut off cob

TEXAS FIELD PEA FRICASSEE

1 tablespoon vegetable oil

1 teaspoon minced garlic
1 shallot, minced
¼ cup julienned leek (white
   portion only)
½ cup finely diced yellow onion
Salt and black pepper to taste
1 cup fresh cut corn
1 cup cooked field peas (lady
   creamer or butter bean)
1 tomato, peeled, seeded and diced
10 tablespoons cold unsalted
   butter, cubed
1 teaspoon chopped fresh herbs

FROM THE CHEF ~ This dish
is probably similar to what the
Native Americans ate centuries
ago. The combination of venison
and corn is truly a native dish.

FOR THE BACON-CORN JOHNNYCAKES

In a large bowl, mix the flours, cornmeal, baking
powder, sugar and salt until well blended. Make a small
well in the center; stir in milk, egg yolk and butter until
well incorporated. In a small sauté pan over medium
heat, render bacon for 2 minutes; add corn and sauté
2 minutes longer. Remove from the heat. In a separate
bowl, whip egg white to a stiff peak. Gently fold into
batter. Fold in bacon and corn (do not overwork).

Heat a greased nonstick pan or griddle over medium-low
heat for about 30 seconds. Drop batter by ¼ cupfuls
onto griddle, leaving room to flip cakes. Cook on low
for 5 minutes or until lightly browned. Turn; cook
2 minutes longer or until done. Keep warm. ▶

FOR THE FRICASSEE

Heat oil in a sauté pan over medium-high heat; sweat the garlic, shallot, leek and onion. Add salt; cook for 2-3 minutes or until tender. Add corn and peas; cook 2 minutes longer. Add tomato; sauté until heated through. Remove from heat; swirl in cold butter. Add herbs, pepper and salt if needed.

FOR THE VENISON

Season the venison loin with Creole seasoning; rub with 2 tablespoons oil. In a large sauté pan, heat remaining oil over high heat to the smoking point. Sear loin for 1-2 minutes on each side. Roast at 400° until internal temperature reaches 120° (roasting time will vary depending on the thickness of the loin). Rest for 10 minutes.

TO PLATE

Shingle two johnnycakes in center of plate; top with a small amount of fricassee. Slice venison into ¼-inch slices; place on top. Finish with remaining fricassee on the side. Serve hot. ■

HUNTING IS VERY POPULAR IN THE SOUTH, and especially in Texas, so it is fitting to have a number of wild game dishes on our menu. Some of the game is truly wild, while some is raised on free-range farms, but with regulated feed. We serve venison, antelope, elk, bison, wild boar, quail, pheasant, chukar and duck. Many of these meats can be used interchangeably with the recipes in the book.

The majority of our game comes from one company in the Texas Hill Country, Broken Arrow Ranch. The Hughes family provides us with venison, antelope and wild boar. These animals forage on nuts and berries, which gives the meat a distinctive flavor profile.

Other game found in the Hill Country are Sika, Axis and Fallow venison, and Nilgai and Blackbuck antelope, which were imported from Asia. The animals are humanely field-harvested and processed under strict regulations, then aged similar to the way beef is aged. This aging process produces more tender and more flavorful meat. The best way of preparing this meat is simply cooking it no higher than medium-rare. The natural sugars in the blood help with the gamey flavor typically associated with wild game.

Our white-meat game birds come from a local farm. O.G. Barrett has been raising bobwhite quails, ringneck pheasants and chukar partridge for over 50 years. He takes pride in his birds and spends many hours managing and giving his birds the highest quality feed. These birds cook quickly, so allow for carry-over cooking to keep them from drying out.

The duck used in this book is White Peking, which originated in China and was brought to Long Island, New York, hence the name Long Island Duck. Not overcooking is also important with duck. Sear the duck skin side down to allow for the fat in the skin to render. This will yield a crispy, tender skin.

The wild game available to the consumer is not the wild game that you or your neighbor has hunted. This game has been fed, harvested and aged with the utmost attention to detail. Don't be afraid of trying something new ... just remember the secret is to not overcook these meats since they are already naturally lean.

VEAL "WELLINGTON"
Serves 4

FROM THE CHEF ~ A classic beef Wellington has been cooked with paté and mushroom duxelles and baked in pastry. We decided to tear down the dish into its primal parts and look at it in a different way. We subsituted pan-seared foie gras for the paté, wild mushroom ragoût for the duxelles and veal for the beef, then serve it on a pastry disk. It's less time-intensive and allows for the premium ingredients to be seen.

1 egg yolk

1 tablespoon cold water

1 sheet puff pastry

4 veal tenderloin medallions
   (4 ounces *each*)

Salt and black pepper to taste

2 tablespoons vegetable oil

½ pound foie gras, cut into
    ½-inch slices
1 recipe Wild Mushroom Ragoût
    (see page 200)
1 cup Marsala Demi-Glace

MARSALA DEMI-GLACE
1 teaspoon butter
1 shallot, roughly chopped
½ teaspoon black peppercorns
½ cup mushroom stems, roughly
    chopped

½ cup Marsala
1 ¼ cups Veal Demi-Glace (recipe
    on page 201)
Salt to taste

FOR THE PUFF PASTRY

In a small bowl, beat egg yolk and water. Cut
cold puff pastry into four 3-inch circles. Place on
a parchment-lined baking sheet. Brush with egg
wash. Bake at 375° for 12 minutes or until golden.
Set aside.

FOR THE DEMI-GLACE

Melt butter in a small saucepan over medium
heat; sweat shallot for 3 minutes or until translucent. Add the peppercorns, mushroom stems
and Marsala. Increase heat and reduce Marsala
until it is almost dry (about 2 tablespoons). Add
demi-glace; simmer for 5 minutes or until mixture
reaches sauce consistency. Strain twice through a
fine mesh strainer. Adjust seasoning. Keep warm,
or cover and store in the refrigerator for 1 week or
freeze up to 6 months.

FOR THE VEAL

Season the veal with salt and pepper. In a medium
sauté pan over high heat, sear veal for 2-3 minutes

on each side. Roast at 375° until internal
temperature reaches 120° or meat reaches desired
doneness. Rest for 5 minutes before serving.

FOR THE FOIE GRAS

Heat a medium sauté pan over high heat until
the pan is smoking. Season foie gras. Once pan
is hot, sear foie gras for 1 minute; turn and sear
1 minute longer. Remove from the heat. Reserve
foie gras fat.

TO PLATE

Place puff pastry round in center of plate; spoon
2 tablespoons ragoût in center of pastry. Top with
the veal medallion, then the foie gras. Drizzle
demi-glace and a little of the reserved foie gras
fat around pastry. ■

TRUFFLE-SCENTED POUSSIN WITH RUTABAGA HASH

Serves 4

FROM THE CHEF ~ If baby rutabaga is available at the market, buy it — the flavor is incomparable. Chestnuts are in season from October to December ... some gourmet shops sell them shelled and frozen out of season.

Poussin is the French term for spring or young chicken. The meat is tender and mild, which allows the truffles to be a superstar in the dish. Truffles can be found canned at specialty markets year-round and fresh seasonally.

4 semi-boneless poussin (10 to 12 ounces *each*)

2 tablespoons cold unsalted butter

1 ounce black truffle, shaved, *divided*

Salt and white pepper to taste

1 tablespoon vegetable oil

1 tablespoon melted butter

1 recipe Rutabaga and Chestnut Hash

1 recipe Perigord Chicken Demi-Glace

RUTABAGA AND CHESTNUT HASH

1½ cups cubed peeled rutabaga (½-inch cubes)

4 teaspoons vegetable oil, *divided*

Salt and white pepper to taste

12 whole chestnuts (in shell)

3 tablespoons Pancetta lardons (¼-inch cubes)
   (recipe on page 77)

1 leek (white portion only), thinly shaved

1 clove garlic, thinly shaved

1 teaspoon minced chives

PERIGORD CHICKEN DEMI-GLACE

½ tablespoon butter

1 tablespoon minced shallot

1 tablespoon minced black truffle

¼ cup brandy

1 cup Chicken Demi-Glace (recipe on page 201)

Salt and white pepper to taste

1 tablespoon cold butter, cubed

FOR THE POUSSIN

Separate the skin from the breast with the tip of your index finger, working gently to not tear the skin. Cut the cold butter into four slices and then in half. Place butter pads and half of the shaved truffle between the skin and breast meat. With the tip of a paring knife, pierce the thigh and make a ½-inch incision. Pull opposite leg through the hole to cross the legs of the poussin. Season with salt and pepper.

Heat oil in a medium sauté pan over medium-high heat; sear the poussin, breast side down, for 2 minutes or until golden. Turn over. Finish cooking in a 400° oven, basting with melted butter every 5 minutes. Roast for 15 minutes or until internal temperature reaches 160°. Remove from the oven and tent with foil to carry over to 165°.

FOR THE HASH

Toss rutabaga with 3 teaspoons oil, salt and pepper. Place on a baking sheet. Bake at 400° for 30 minutes or until tender and slightly browned. With the tip of a paring knife, score an X into the flatter side of each chestnut. Arrange on a baking sheet with scored side facing up. Roast at 400° ▶

for 20 minutes or until tender and easily peeled. *(When peeling the hot chestnuts, wear a double layer of latex gloves.)*

Heat remaining oil in a medium sauté pan over medium heat; render pancetta until crispy. Use a slotted spoon to remove to a small bowl. In the drippings, sauté leek and garlic over medium-high heat for 2 minutes or until garlic begins to brown slightly. Add warm rutabaga, chestnuts and pancetta. Adjust seasoning and add chives.

FOR THE DEMI-GLACE

Melt butter in a small saucepan over medium heat; sweat shallot and truffle for 2 minutes. Flame with brandy and reduce by two-thirds. Add demi-glace; simmer for 10-15 minutes or until mixture reaches sauce consistency. Adjust seasoning. Remove from the heat; whisk in cold butter.

TO PLATE

Place hash on plate; top with poussin. Spoon demi-glace around it; sprinkle with remaining truffle. ■

DUCK POT PIE

Serves 4

¼ cup vegetable oil

2 teaspoons minced garlic

¼ cup finely diced sweet onion

2 tablespoons finely diced leek (white portion only)

½ cup sliced shiitake mushroom caps

¼ cup finely diced carrot

¼ cup finely diced celeriac

¼ cup finely diced fennel bulb

¼ cup fresh field peas

2 tablespoons minced celery

2 tablespoons white wine

¼ cup flour

3 cups Duck Stock (recipe on page 201) or low-sodium chicken broth

Salt and black pepper to taste

1 cup Duck Confit (recipe on page 200)

1 tablespoon minced chives

1 egg yolk

1 tablespoon cold water

2 sheets puff pastry

FROM THE CHEF ~ This is my favorite dish on a rainy or cold day. Feel free to substitute your favorite game bird for the duck. For the fresh peas, use black-eyed, purple hull or lady creamers.

FOR THE FILLING

Heat oil in a saucepan over medium heat; sauté garlic, onion and leek for 3-4 minutes to caramelize slightly. Add the remaining vegetables; sauté 4 minutes longer. Deglaze pan with wine; allow to evaporate until almost dry. Stir in the flour; cook for 2 minutes. Stir in stock. Bring to a boil; reduce to a fast simmer. Simmer for 30-45 minutes or until peas are tender. Adjust seasonings. Add confit and chives; heat through.

FOR THE PUFF PASTRY VOL-AU-VENT

For egg wash, beat egg yolk with water. Cut cold puff pastry into eight 4-inch circles. Working quickly, cut a 2-inch circle from the center of four pastries. (If the pastry gets warm, place in the freezer for 10 minutes.) Brush the 4-inch disks with egg wash; top with puff pastry rings. Brush edges and 2-inch disks with egg wash. Place on a baking sheet. Bake at 375° for 12 minutes or until golden.

TO PLATE

Ladle 2 ounces of sauce from filling into a shallow bowl. Place puff pastry cup in the center of the sauce; spoon filling into cup. Top with 2-inch pastry disk. ∎

TEXAS BOBWHITE QUAIL WITH HONEY-BALSAMIC GASTRIQUE

Serves 8

FROM THE CHEF ~ Gastrique is classically caramelized sugar with vinegar added to make a sweet-and-sour sauce. I had the idea for this dish for a PBS series called *At the Chef's Table*.

Besides the astounding flavor, the presentation of this dish is unbelievable. Guests are amazed to see the honeycomb crushed and combined with the balsamic.

2 tablespoons vegetable oil, *divided*

½ cup diced yellow onion

¼ cup diced celery

¼ cup diced carrot

1 tablespoon diced jalapeño

2 ancho chiles

10 arbol chiles

½ apple, diced

Peel of ½ lemon

1 clove garlic, crushed

1 bag Zatarain's Crab Boil

1 tablespoon Louisiana hot sauce

1 tablespoon Worcestershire sauce

6½ cups water, *divided*

2 cups ice

¼ cup salt

¼ cup honey

8 semi-boneless bobwhite quail

1 tablespoon butter

1 recipe Apple-Beet Salad

APPLE-BEET SALAD

2 large beets

1 tablespoon olive oil

Salt and black pepper to taste

1 Granny Smith apple

½ cup micro celery

¼ cup Spiced Pecans (recipe on page 199)

1 tablespoon olive oil

1 teaspoon aged balsamic vinegar

Salt and black pepper to taste

GARNISH

8 honeycomb cubes (½-inch cubes)

¼ cup aged balsamic vinegar

FOR THE QUAIL

Heat 1 tablespoon oil in a large saucepan over medium heat; add the next nine ingredients and sweat for 3 minutes. Add crab boil, hot sauce; Worcestershire sauce and 2½ cups water. Simmer for 30 minutes. Remove from the heat. Place salt and honey in a large container. Strain hot liquid into container; stir to dissolve salt and honey. Add ice and remaining water. Place quail in brine in the refrigerator for 8 hours or overnight.

Remove quail from brine. With the tip of a paring knife, pierce the thigh and make a ½-inch incision. Pull opposite leg through the hole to cross the legs of the quail. Heat remaining oil in a medium sauté pan over medium-high heat; sear the quail for 1 minute on all sides, basting with butter while searing. Bake at 400° for 4-5 minutes. Remove from the oven and allow to rest.

FOR THE SALAD

Wash beets thoroughly and remove tops. Cut off both ends. Place each beet on a 6-inch square of foil. Drizzle with oil; sprinkle with salt and pepper. Seal foil; bake at 400° for 45-60 minutes or until a knife slides through the beets easily. While still hot, rub beets with a towel to remove skin; cool. With a mandoline, julienne the beets and apple. Toss with celery, pecans, oil and vinegar; season to taste.

TO PLATE

Slice quail breast into three ¼-inch slices; fan out in the center of an oval plate. Place a tuft of salad alongside; center honeycomb between the salad and quail. Drizzle balsamic over honeycomb and quail. At the table, crush the honeycomb with the back of a spoon to create the gastrique. ■

BLACK LACQUERED DUCK
Serves 4

FROM THE CHEF ~ Duck, orange and foie gras are just meant to be together. By salting the duck, you remove the water in the typically chewy skin, then allow it to absorb the honey. Once roasted, the skin is sweet and crispy. The foie gras bombe can be served alone as an appetizer. The demi-glace is a take on our tableside flaming café brûlot, made with chicory coffee and orange and lemon peel.

2 ducks (4 to 5 pounds *each*), leg quarters
   removed and held for confit
4 cups kosher salt
2 cups honey
1 recipe Foie Gras Bombe
1 recipe Satsuma-Chicory Demi-Glace

FOIE GRAS BOMBE

1 bunch red Swiss chard
6 tablespoons butter, cubed, *divided*
Salt and white pepper to taste
1 leek (white portion only), sliced
¼ cup water
1 cup Duck Confit (recipe on page 200)
½ teaspoon chopped fresh herbs
¼ pound foie gras, cut into ½-inch cubes

SATSUMA-CHICORY DEMI-GLACE

½ tablespoon unsalted butter
1 tablespoon minced shallot
1 teaspoon black peppercorns
¼ cup Grand Marnier
½ cup satsuma juice or strained fresh orange juice
1 tablespoon chicory coffee

1 cup Veal Demi-Glace (recipe on page 201)
Kosher salt to taste
Zest of 1 satsuma orange
½ teaspoon lemon juice

FOR THE DUCK

Rub ducks thoroughly with kosher salt; cut off the tail to allow drainage. Place on a rack in a shallow pan. Refrigerate for 24 hours. Under cold running water, wash ducks to remove salt and any excess fat from skin.

In a large stockpot over high heat, bring 2 gallons of water to a boil. Stir in honey. Submerge ducks for 3 minutes. Drain and place on a wire rack in a high-sided roasting pan. Roast at 500° for 10 minutes. Refrigerate until cooled.

Carve each breast as a whole piece from the carcass. Heat a sauté pan over high heat; sear duck breast, skin side down, for 1 minute. Then roast, skin side down, at 400° for 10 minutes. Remove from the pan and rest.

FOR THE BOMBE

Remove leaves from chard; finely chop stalks to yield ¼ cup and set aside. In a saucepan, bring 4 cups salted water to a boil. Cook chard leaves for 15 seconds; shock in ice water. In a small sauté pan over medium heat, melt 2 tablespoons butter. Add chopped chard stalks; season with salt and pepper. Sweat for 4 minutes or until tender; drain on paper towel.

In a small sauté pan over medium heat, melt remaining butter; add leeks, salt, pepper and water. ▶

Increase heat to a fast simmer; cook until leeks are tender and water is nearly evaporated. Swirl the pan in a rapid motion to help emulsify the butter and remaining water. This is important; otherwise, the butter will give the leeks a greasy appearance. Set aside.

Season foie gras cubes with salt and pepper. Heat another small sauté pan over high heat. Once pan is extremely hot, add foie gras and quickly sear on all sides. Remove from the heat.

FOR THE CONFIT

Remove duck skin; pull the meat, being cautious to remove all of the bones. In a small sauté pan over medium heat, heat 1 tablespoon reserved confit fat. Add duck meat and herbs; heat through.

FOR THE DEMI-GLACE

Heat butter in a small saucepan over medium heat; sweat shallot for 3 minutes or until translucent. Add peppercorns, Grand Marnier, juice and coffee; reduce by two-thirds. Add demi-glace; simmer for 20 minutes or until mixture reaches sauce consistency. Strain twice through a fine mesh strainer. Add orange zest; adjust seasoning with salt and lemon juice. Keep warm.

TO ASSMEBLE THE BOMBE

Line 2½-inch metal rings (or biscuit cutters) with blanched chard leaves; use enough chard so the leaves line the entire ring with about a 1½-inch overhang. Fill rings evenly with foie gras, leeks, sautéed chard stalks and confit, tightly packing each layer. Fold chard leaves over confit to form small cylindrical packages.

Add water to a low-sided sauté pan, filling a quarter of the way up the sides; bring to a simmer. Using a spatula, place rings in simmering water. (The water should come about ½ inch up the ring.) Cover pan with a parchment round. Bake at 400° for 8-10 minutes.

TO PLATE

Turn the hot bombe onto the upper center of the plate, allowing for the solid chard leaf to be visible. Remove the ring. Slice duck breast into ¼-inch slices. Fan the slices, skin side up, around two-thirds of the ring. Finish with a drizzling of demi-glace. ■

RABBIT THREE WAYS
Serves 4

2 whole rabbits

Salt and white pepper to taste

2 tablespoons vegetable oil

BRAISED RABBIT

4 rabbit hindquarters, thigh
   bone removed

Salt and white pepper to taste

2 tablespoons vegetable oil

½ cup diced yellow onion

¼ cup diced carrot

¼ cup diced celery

¼ cup dry sherry

4 cups Rabbit Stock (recipe on
   page 201)

RABBIT CONFIT

4 rabbit forequarters

1 tablespoon kosher salt

1 tablespoon black peppercorns

4 sprigs thyme

4 cloves garlic

1 tablespoon juniper berries, crushed

2 bay leaves

2 shallots, sliced

2 cups olive oil

BARLEY RISOTTO

6 tablespoons butter, *divided*

½ cup finely diced yellow onion

2 green garlic bulbs, shaved
   and tops bias cut

2 cups pearl barley

7 cups hot Rabbit Stock (recipe on
   page 201), vegetable stock
   or water

Reserved rabbit confit, pulled

Salt and white pepper to taste

1 teaspoon chopped fresh herbs
   (thyme, basil and oregano)

FROM THE CHEF ~ The unique thing about this dish is serving an unusual ingredient three ways — a rack of rabbit, braised rabbit hindquarters and a confit made from the forequarters. For ease of preparation, remove the loin without the bones.

You can use the same method in preparing the barley for any other starchy grain, like Israeli couscous or Arborio rice. Pearl barley is available in many supermarkets and specialty food stores.

FOR THE BRAISED RABBIT

Season hindquarters with salt and pepper. Heat oil over high heat in a large saucepan; sear rabbit on all sides for 2 minutes or until golden brown. Remove. In the same pan, sauté onion, carrot and celery over medium-high heat for 3-4 minutes or until caramelized. Deglaze pan with sherry. Add stock. Return rabbit to the pan. Bring to a simmer. Cover and braise in a 300° oven for 6 hours or until meat is tender.

Remove rabbit to a separate pan and cover. Strain braising liquid twice through a fine mesh strainer. Allow to settle for 5 minutes; skim fat. Reduce stock by half and adjust seasoning; set aside.

FOR THE CONFIT

Place forequarters in a square baking dish with high sides; season liberally with salt. Add peppercorns, thyme, ▶

garlic, juniper berries, bay leaves and shallots; toss. Cover with plastic wrap and refrigerate overnight.

Remove dish from refrigerator. Cover rabbit with oil, plastic wrap and foil. Bake at 250° for 2-3 hours or until meat is falling off the bones. Allow rabbit to cool in the fat.

FOR THE RISOTTO

Melt 4 tablespoons butter in a 4- to 5-quart sauce-pan over medium heat. Add onion and shaved garlic bulbs; cook for 4-5 minutes or until translu-cent. (Reduce heat if the onion begins to brown.) Add barley; cook over medium heat, stirring constantly, for about 4 minutes. (Adjust the heat as necessary; the barley needs to be toasted, but not browned.)

Add 1½ cups of hot stock or water, stirring con-stantly. The barley mixture will look a bit watery. As it begins to cook, stir constantly, making sure to scrape along the bottom of the pan so it doesn't stick. When most of the liquid is absorbed and the barley begins to look a bit dry, add another 1½ cups of hot stock and stir constantly as before. At this point, the risotto can be poured onto a sheet pan and refrigerated until needed, or you can continue with the process if serving immediately.

In a medium saucepan, heat reserved confit and remaining butter. Add the parcooked risotto and fold in the confit; add the remaining hot stock until you have used most of it. Adjust seasoning with salt, pepper and garlic tops. When the barley is tender and the risotto has a creamy consistency,

almost like thick oatmeal, it is done. (To test, bite into a pearl of barley. It should be tender without being too mushy. If it is still crunchy and tastes a bit starchy, you will need to continue adding liquid and cooking further.)

FOR THE RACK OF RABBIT

Remove the quarters of the whole rabbits with a sharp knife and reserve; cut through the sternum. Cut carefully down the spine from shoulder to hip, removing the loin and leaving the rib cage attached. Remove belly meat from the loin, leaving the ribs attached to loin. Cut cartilage from the ribs, exposing the rib bones. Scrape the back of the ribs with the knife blade. Carefully peel the meat around the ribs to the loin and trim away the meat. (The loin should still be attached to the clean ribs.) Fold the loin in half in front of the ribs; using butcher's twine, tie the loin to the ribs. (It should have the appearance of a cleaned rack of meat.) Wrap the exposed bones with foil.

Season with salt and pepper. Heat oil in a medium sauté pan over high heat; sear the rack of rabbit for 2 minutes on each side. Finish in a 400° oven for 5 minutes to cook the rabbit throughout. Remove from oven and let rest.

TO PLATE

Spoon risotto onto the upper right side of the plate; lean braised hindquarter against risotto. Remove twine from rack of rabbit and cut in half. Place the rack in front of the risotto with cut sides facing out. Pour a little of the braising sauce on and around the rabbit. ■

Confit of Berkshire Pork with Sweet Potato Spaetzle

Serves 4

FROM THE CHEF ~ I like to keep the fat cap on the rack, so while it cures overnight, the salt pulls out the water in the fat, while the sugar helps push in the flavor from the pickling spices. Once the water has been extracted, frying the pork will crisp the fat like crackling. It's a great combination of crunchy and rich, moist meat.

3 tablespoons pickling spices or
   Zatarain's crab boil in a bag
2 tablespoons salt
1 tablespoon granulated sugar
1 Berkshire pork rack (3 pounds and
   4 bone), french with fat cap on
Lard for frying
2 cups Sweet Potato Spaetzle
1 recipe Savoy Cabbage Slaw
1 recipe Steen's Sugarcane Barbecue Demi-Glace

SWEET POTATO SPAETZLE

3 eggs
1 tablespoon heavy whipping cream
5 teaspoons melted butter
½ teaspoon salt
1⅓ cups hot sweet potato pulp
   (1 large sweet potato)
1½ cups all-purpose flour
1 tablespoon vegetable oil
2 tablespoons butter
¼ cup brunoise sweet potato
1 teaspoon chopped parsley
Salt and black pepper to taste

SAVOY CABBAGE SLAW

½ cup julienned sweet onion
½ cup sugarcane vinegar
2 cups shredded savoy cabbage
¼ cup julienned red bell pepper
Salt and black pepper to taste

STEEN'S SUGARCANE BARBECUE DEMI-GLACE

¼ cup Steen's sugarcane syrup
2 tablespoons yellow mustard
2 tablespoons Steen's sugarcane vinegar
1 tablespoon Worcestershire sauce
1 tablespoon Louisiana hot sauce
Salt to taste
1 cup Veal Demi-Glace (recipe on page 201) ▶

Photo on page 135

In a coffee grinder, process the pickling spices, salt and sugar to a fine grind. Rub into the pork rack; wrap in plastic wrap. Refrigerate overnight.

In a mixing bowl, combine the eggs, cream, melted butter, salt and sweet potato pulp. Mix in flour to form dough (you may need a little more or less flour depending on the moisture content of the sweet potato).

Bring a saucepan of salted water to a boil. Use a colander or spaetzle maker to push the dough into the simmering water; cook for 2 minutes. Once the spaetzle begin to float, remove with a slotted spoon to a bowl of ice water. Once chilled, strain spaetzle through a colander. Toss with oil; cover and refrigerate for up to 2 days.

In a bowl, marinate the onion in vinegar for 1 hour or until tender. Add the cabbage, bell pepper, salt and pepper; toss. Marinate for 5 minutes. (Marinate longer for a softer slaw; I like the crispness of the cabbage to pair with the soft pillows of spaetzle.)

Heat a saucepan over medium heat; stir in the syrup, mustard, vinegar, Worcestershire sauce, hot sauce and salt. Bring to a boil; cook for 5 minutes.

Add demi-glace; simmer for 15 minutes or until sauce coats the back of a spoon. Keep warm until serving, or cover and store in the refrigerator for up to 1 week.

In a deep fryer or high-sided stockpot, heat lard to 365°. Slice pork rack into four chops, leaving the fat cap on. Place chops in a fryer basket and carefully lower into lard. Cook for 10-15 minutes or until internal temperature reaches a minimum of 140°. Drain on a wire rack for 5 minutes before serving.

Heat a sauté pan over medium heat. Add 2 tablespoons butter and brunoise sweet potato; cook for 2-3 minutes or until the potato begins to soften. Add spaetzle, parsley, salt and pepper; heat through.

Place a mound of slaw on plate at the 11 o'clock position; place ½ cup spaetzle to the right of the slaw. With a sharp knife, cut three horizontal ⅛-inch slices from the middle of each pork chop. Lean against the slaw so the bone is in the air and the slices are fanned out. Pour 3 tablespoons demi-glace over pork and around the plate. ■

SOUTHERN COMFORT SHORT RIBS WITH PORK AND BEANS

Serves 4

1 recipe Southern Comfort Marinade

4 beef short ribs (2-inch kosher cut),
    bones removed and reserved

2 tablespoons vegetable oil

½ cup diced yellow onion

¼ cup diced carrot

¼ cup diced celery

4 cups Veal Stock (recipe on
    page 201)

1 recipe Pork and Beans

SOUTHERN COMFORT MARINADE

1 cup Southern Comfort

2 cups Coke

3 cups water

8 cloves garlic, crushed

3 sprigs thyme

½ tablespoon kosher salt

1 tablespoon black peppercorns

PORK AND BEANS

2 tablespoons vegetable oil

¼ pound Pancetta (recipe on
    page 77), diced

2 teaspoons minced garlic

1 shallot, minced

1 leek (white portion only), chopped

2 cups fresh pinto or butter beans

½ cup braising liquid

5 cups water

6 tablespoons unsalted butter, cubed

2 tablespoons chopped green onions

FROM THE CHEF ~ Rolling the boneless short ribs is for presentation. You can leave the bone in and prepare the recipe in the same manner with the ribs lying flat. Fresh beans are the best for this dish.

FOR THE SHORT RIBS

Combine marinade ingredients in a nonreactive pan. Add ribs. Cover and refrigerate overnight. Drain and reserve marinade. Roll each rib into itself to form a cylinder; truss with butcher's twine.

Heat oil over high heat in a large saucepan; sear ribs on all sides for 1½ minutes or until golden brown. Remove. In the same pan, sauté onion, carrot and celery over medium-high heat for 3-4 minutes or until caramelized. Add reserved beef bones. Deglaze pan with reserved marinade. Add veal stock. Return ribs to the pan. Bring to a simmer. Cover and braise in a 300° oven for 5 hours or until meat is tender.

Remove ribs to a separate pan and cover. Strain braising liquid through a fine mesh strainer. Allow to settle for 5 minutes; skim fat. Adjust seasoning and reserve. Or pour over ribs; cover and refrigerate for up to 3 days. ▶

Heat oil in a saucepan over medium-high heat; render pancetta for 2 minutes. Add garlic, shallot and leek; sauté for 3-4 minutes. Add beans, braising liquid and water. Bring to a boil; reduce to a fast simmer. Simmer for 1 to 1½ hours or until beans are tender and have a creamy inner texture.

TO PLATE

Add ribs to the beans and heat through. Once the ribs are hot, remove to a plate. Finish beans over medium heat by swirling in the cold butter; stir in green onions. Adjust seasonings. Ladle beans into a bowl; place a rib in the center of the bowl. ∎

2 tablespoons vegetable oil

1 recipe Blue Cheese Lyonnaise Potatoes

BLUE CHEESE LYONNAISE POTATOES

8 fingerling potatoes

2 tablespoons unsalted butter

½ medium yellow onion, julienned

1½ tablespoons minced garlic

1½ tablespoons flour

½ cup brandy

1½ cups whole milk

⅓ cup good-quality blue cheese

Frying oil

Fresh herbs to taste

Salt and white pepper to taste

COCOA NIB-CRUSTED CHÂTEAUBRIAND
Serves 4

FROM THE CHEF ~ Cocoa nibs are the purest form of chocolate. These raw cocoa beans have some of the same bitter flavors as black pepper and coffee, which are often used with Châteaubriand, so I decided to give it a try. I ended up with a great crust that has a underlying chocolate note, which pairs well with the saltiness of the blue cheese.

¼ cup cocoa nibs

½ teaspoon black peppercorns

2 teaspoons salt

1 center-cut tenderloin of beef (1½ pounds), trimmed

FOR THE CHÂTEAUBRIAND

In a coffee grinder, process the cocoa nibs and peppercorns to a medium grind; add salt. Rub into the tenderloin. Heat oil in a large sauté pan over high heat; sear tenderloin for 2 minutes on each side. Roast at 400° for 12-18 minutes or until the internal temperature reaches 120°. Let rest for 10 minutes.

FOR THE POTATOES

Place potatoes in a large pot; cover with cold water. Bring to a boil; cook until fork-tender. Drain and cool. Melt butter in a saucepan over medium-high heat; sauté onion and garlic for 3 minutes. Stir in the flour to make a roux. Deglaze pan with brandy. Reduce heat and add the milk; bring to a simmer. Over low heat, slowly melt blue cheese into milk mixture. Keep warm. ▶

Cut cooled potatoes lengthwise in half. Heat oil to 375°; fry potatoes until golden brown and crispy. Toss with herbs, salt and pepper, then toss with cheese sauce.

Slice tenderloin into ¼-inch slices. Spoon the Lyonnaise potatoes in the center of the plate; shingle beef slices over potatoes. Drizzle remaining blue cheese sauce over and around beef. ▪

PURPLE HAZE SOUFFLÉ

FLEUR-DE-LIS FROMAGE
WITH CAVIAR

EWE'S BLUE WITH
SECKLE PEAR

BRÛLÉE OF APPALACHIAN
JACK

SUPER AGED GOUDA FONDUE

CHEESE — A FEW YEARS AGO,

we noticed the beginning of something new — small farms in little towns around America producing cheeses with great characteristics and the quality of those made for centuries in Europe. We started building relationships with these artisans, and over time they understood our passion. It is the same passion they have for their cheese.

These cheese makers gave us the opportunity to let us try new products that they only made in small quantities for themselves. We are one of the lucky few to be allowed to experience these experimental cheeses. What we are offering you is a chance to try a little bit of passion ... ours and theirs.

creating your own cheese plate

I GREW UP THINKING A CHEESE PLATTER to entertain company meant cheese in a can and crackers. That idea has certainly changed.

The first step to creating a cheese board is choosing the cheese. Selecting an artisan product is an important detail that should not be overlooked. Cheeses that are hand-made with quality ingredients are preferred over those that are factory made and marked with a sticker to assure you it truly is cheese.

Variety is the spice of life, and cheese is no different. Variety means many things when it comes to cheese. Cheese can be categorized by the type of milk (from cows, goats or sheep) …

the texture of the cheese (soft, creamy, semi-firm or hard) … the age of the cheese … and the style in which it ripened.

I recommend three to five cheeses on a cheese board. I prefer having at least one cow's milk cheese, one goat's milk cheese and one sheep's milk cheese with varying styles — a soft-ripened cheese or triple cream cheese, a washed-rind cheese to give a punch to the plat-ter, an aged cheese that is sharp and condensed in flavor, and finally a blue cheese.

For a course with dinner, plan on 3 ounces per person. When cheese is the only food offered, plan on 5 ounces. Cheese should be served at 65° to 68° to let the

flavors and aroma come out. Remove cheese from the refrig-erator an hour before serving.

For garnishes and accompani-ments, many foods go well with cheese, such as fruits (both dry and fresh), nuts, baguettes and my favorite — honeycomb. A combination is a good way to go, since different cheeses go better with different sides.

Remember, cheese is living and changes every day just as wine changes. Try new cheeses that might challenge your palate. Write tasting notes of the cheeses you like and search out that style of cheese from a different producer.

Just smile and say cheese!

PURPLE HAZE SOUFFLÉ

Serves 6

FROM THE CHEF ~ Many people are afraid of soufflés because they are so temperamental. The choux paste works as a matrix to hold the egg whites by allowing the soufflé to rise without billing. Think of this soufflé as a strata of choux, egg white, choux, egg white and so on.

CHOUX PASTE

7 tablespoons all-purpose flour

3 ounces unsalted butter, softened

2 cups milk

1/8 teaspoon lavender

5 ounces Cypress Grove Purple Haze
   Goat Cheese (see page 147)

2 egg yolks

SAUCE

1¾ cups Choux Paste

1½ cups milk

1 cup heavy whipping cream

3 ounces plain goat cheese

Salt and black pepper to taste

SOUFFLÉ

1½ cup egg whites

½ teaspoon iodized salt

1 teaspoon sugar

1½ cups Choux Paste

FOR THE CHOUX PASTE

In a mixing bowl, thoroughly combine flour and butter. In a saucepan, bring the milk, lavender and cheese to a boil. Whisk in the butter mixture. Bring to a simmer and continue to stir for 2 minutes. Remove from the heat; quickly whisk in the egg yolks. Stir to keep the yolks from scrambling.

FOR THE SAUCE

In a saucepan, combine the sauce ingredients. Cook and stir over high heat until sauce comes to a simmer. Adjust seasoning and adjust thickness with milk as needed. Keep warm.

FOR THE SOUFFLÉ

In a stand mixer, whip egg whites to soft peaks. Add salt and sugar; beat to stiff peaks. Place choux paste in a mixing bowl; add a third of the whipped egg whites. Combine to loosen the paste. Gently fold in remaining egg whites. Do not overwork; not all the paste needs to be incorporated. Transfer to greased ramekins or soufflé cups, filling to the top. Using your finger, release the egg white mixture from the sides. Bake at 400° for 18 minutes or until golden brown.

TO PLATE

Remove soufflé from oven to a base plate; pour sauce into middle of soufflé and serve immediately. ∎

FLEUR-DE-LIS FROMAGE TRIPLE CREAM CHEESE WITH PETROSSIAN CAVIAR

Serves 8

2 tablespoons finely minced shallot

2 tablespoons finely minced chives

1 recipe Blue Corn Blini

2 ounces (60 grams) American
    Sturgeon caviar

1 Fleur-de-Lis Fromage Triple Cream
    Cheese, cut into 8 wedges

BLUE CORN BLINI

1 package active dry yeast

1½ cups warm milk (108° to 110°)

1 cup blue corn flour

½ cup all-purpose flour

1 teaspoon sugar

½ teaspoon salt

¼ cup unsalted butter, melted

3 eggs, *separated*

FROM THE CHEF ~ Fleur-de-lis Fromage Triple Cream Cheese, made by Bittersweet Plantation Dairy in Louisiana (see information on page 147), has won many awards worldwide. I use this cheese as my crème fraîche to accompany the caviar. To order or to learn more about Petrossian caviar, see the Source Guide on page 204.

FOR THE BLINI

In a large bowl, proof yeast with warm milk for 10 minutes, stirring to dissolve. In another large bowl, sift together the flours, sugar and salt. Make a well in the center; pour in the yeast mixture, butter and egg yolks. Whisk until smooth. Cover with a towel and let rise in a warm place for 1½ hours.

Just before you are ready to cook the blini, whip the egg whites in a stand mixer until stiff, then fold into the batter. Pour 1 tablespoon of batter onto a lightly greased griddle over medium-high heat. Cook for 30 seconds on each side. Repeat with remaining batter. Stack the blini on a platter and wrap in a cloth napkin to keep warm.

TO PLATE

Combine the shallot and chives. Place a short stack of three blinis off-center on each plate; top with a teaspoonful of shallot mixture. Spoon a ½-ounce quenelle of caviar on one side of blinis and place a wedge of cheese on the other side. ∎

EWE'S BLUE WITH SECKLE PEAR

Serves 4

FROM THE CHEF ~ Ewe's Blue is a Roquefort-style cheese with a creamy texture from Old Chatham Sheepherding Co. (see information on page 147). The stuffed pears can be served at room temperature if desired instead of warmed ... let them sit out, covered, for 1 hour before serving.

4 underripe Seckle pears

1½ cups Zinfandel

1 teaspoon Szechuan pepper berry

2 whole cloves

¼ split vanilla bean, scraped

¼ cup Ewe's Blue

1 cup baby greens

2 tablespoons Dried Cherry Vinaigrette

DRIED CHERRY VINAIGRETTE

½ cup dried tart cherries

¼ cup julienned yellow onion

½ cup champagne or sparkling wine

¼ split vanilla bean, scraped

3 tablespoons red wine vinegar

6 tablespoons vegetable oil

½ teaspoon chopped fresh herbs

Salt and black pepper to taste

FOR THE PEARS

Peel pears, leaving stems intact. Using a parisienne scoop (melon baller), core pear from the bottom so it is hollowed out. Trim bottom so pear will sit flat. In a 1-quart saucepan, combine the wine, pepper berry, cloves and vanilla bean. Bring to a simmer over medium-high heat; reduce heat to low. Add pears; poach for 5 minutes or until almost tender. Refrigerate in poaching liquid. Once cool, remove from liquid and drain. Stuff pears with cheese. Chill until serving.

FOR THE VINAIGRETTE

In a small saucepan, combine cherries, onion, champagne and vanilla bean. Bring to a boil over medium-high heat; cook until most of the champagne is absorbed. Remove from the heat; remove vanilla bean. In a food processor, pulse cherry mixture, leaving it chunky. Add vinegar, oil and herbs; pulse a few times. Season with salt and pepper. Cover and refrigerate.

TO PLATE

Warm the stuffed pears in a 350° oven for 5 minutes. In a small mixing bowl, toss the greens with vinaigrette. Place a pear in the center of each plate; place a mound of greens behind and to the left of pear. Use a slotted spoon to remove some cherries from vinaigrette and place in front of greens. ■

Photo on page 140

Bittersweet Plantation
2517 South Philippe Ave.
Gonzales LA 70737
225.644.6000
www.jfolse.com/bittersweet_dairy

Cypress Grove
1330 Q Street
Arcata CA 95521
707.825.1100
www.cypressgrovechevre.com

Bobolink Dairy
42 Meadowburn Road
Vernon NJ 07462
973.764.4888
www.cowsoutside.com

Meadow Creek Dairy
6724 Meadow Creek Road
Galax VA 24333
888.236.0622
www.meadowcreekdairy.com

Carr Valley Cheese Company
S3797 County G
La Valle WI 53941
800.462.7258
www.carrvalleycheese.com

Old Chatham Sheepherding Co.
155 Shaker Museum Road
Old Chatham NY 12136
888.743.3760
www.blacksheepcheese.com

Cato Corner Farm
178 Cato Corner Road
Colchester CT 06415
860.537.3884
www.catocornerfarm.com

Pure Luck Texas
101 Twin Oaks Trail
Dripping Springs TX 78620
512.858.7034
www.purelucktexas.com

Cheesemakers Inc.
2266 South Walker Road
Cleveland TX 77328
866.593.1319
www.cheesemakers.com

Westfield Farm
28 Worcester Road
Hubbardston MA 01452
877.777.3900
www.chevre.com

Cowgirl Creamery
80 Fourth Street
Point Reyes Station CA 94956
866.433.7834
www.cowgirlcreamery.com

Winchester Cheese Company
32605 Holland Road
Winchester CA 92596
951.926.4239
www.winchestercheese.com

BRÛLÉE OF APPALACHIAN JACK
Serves 4

2 tablespoons raw sugar

¼ pound Meadow Creek Dairy Appalachian Jack
 (see page 147), cut into 4 triangles

¼ pound venison pastrami, thinly sliced

1 recipe Apple-Pecan Confiture

¼ ounce micro greens

2 tablespoons aged balsamic vinegar

APPLE-PECAN CONFITURE

1 Granny Smith apple, peeled, cored and quartered

1 shallot, peeled and quartered

1 cup vegetable oil

¼ cup toasted pecans

Salt to taste

FOR THE CONFITURE

In a small saucepan over medium heat, cook the apple and shallot in oil for 15 minutes or until tender. Drain. In a food processor, pulse the pecans until finely ground. Add cooked apple and shallot; purée until smooth. Adjust seasoning with a touch of salt. Refrigerate in a covered container for up to 3 days.

TO PLATE

Sprinkle a thin sheet of sugar over the cheese triangles. Using a blow torch, burn sugar as you would for crème brûlée; sprinkle with remaining sugar and burn a second time. Arrange pastrami slices on plate, creating a mound. Lay cheese triangles against pastrami. Place a small amount of confiture next to the cheese. Finish with a tuft of micro greens and a drizzling of balsamic vinegar. ■

BOERE KAAS SUPER AGED GOUDA FONDUE
Serves 4-6

FROM THE CHEF ~ Any variety of hard cheese can be used for this recipe, but I wanted to highlight the Dutch influence of the Boere Kaas Super Aged Gouda from Winchester Cheese Company. It's intensely sharp and dry, so a beer with sweet notes — such as a Trappist ale or bock — will help balance the fondue. Serve with Holland Rye or another intensely flavored rye bread, and you'll have a big, bold cheese course.

2 tablespoons unsalted butter

1 tablespoon minced garlic

1 tablespoon flour

¼ cup beer (microbrew with a hint of sweetness)

½ cup whole milk

½ cup shredded Super Aged Gouda

Salt and white pepper to taste

In a small saucepan, melt butter. Add garlic; cook for 2 minutes on medium-low heat. Stir in flour to make a roux; cook for 4-5 minutes, stirring continuously. Deglaze the pan with beer. Increase heat and add the milk. Bring to a boil. Reduce heat to low; slowly stir in cheese. Season with salt and pepper. Transfer to a fondue pot; keep warm. Serve with bread or fresh vegetables. ■

DESSERT — DESSERTS MAY BE THE BIGGEST challenge for the Kitchen Table. When people come to Brennan's, there are certain dishes that are must-haves, such as Bananas Foster. So we decided to give them what they want, but surprise them with new desserts they may never order in the dining room.

We call our dessert course at the Kitchen Table the "Bomb"— there are more desserts than anyone could imagine eating. Some are standards, while others are seasonal, but with desserts, it's all about memory. Who doesn't have a great memory of roasting marshmallows for a s'more over a campfire?

CHOCOLATE S'MORES

BIT-O-HONEY BEEHIVES

STRAWBERRY & BASIL SOUP

RUSTIC FIG TART

PEANUT BUTTER CUP

PEACH UPSIDE-DOWN CAKES

VANILLA BEAN POUND CAKE

MEYER LEMON SPICE CAKES

RICE CRÈME CARAMEL

CREOLE CRÊPES

CHOCOLATE S'MORES

Serves 16

FROM THE CHEF ~ I came up with this recipe after our wine guy received a s'more maker for Christmas. The following week I had s'mores on the brain, and a few days later, this was on the Kitchen Table dessert menu.

CHOCOLATE MOUSSE

¼ pound 70% chocolate (El Rey)

¼ pound semisweet chocolate

2 tablespoons unsalted butter

¾ cup heavy whipping cream

4 eggs, *separated*

1 teaspoon Jack Daniels

3 tablespoons granulated sugar

½ teaspoon cream of tartar

⅛ teaspoon salt

GRAHAM CRACKER COOKIE*

6 ounces confectioners' sugar

3 ounces cake flour

1 ounce bread flour

1½ ounces graham cracker crumbs

6 egg whites

½ cup butter, melted

1¼ teaspoons vanilla extract

MARSHMALLOW

1 cup confectioners' sugar

1½ tablespoons unflavored powdered gelatin

¾ cup water, *divided*

1 cup granulated sugar

2 tablespoons corn syrup

⅛ teaspoon salt

6 egg whites

FOR THE MOUSSE

Melt chocolate and butter over a water bath just until chocolate is melted (do not overheat). While chocolate is melting, whip cream to soft peaks in a mixing bowl; set aside. In another mixing bowl, whip egg yolks until light and fluffy. Stir in Jack Daniels and incorporate melted chocolate. Fold in whipped cream.

Whip egg whites; once they become aerated, add sugar, cream of tartar and salt. Continue to whip to stiff peaks. Add a fourth of the egg whites to the chocolate mixture to lighten, then fold in remaining whites until just combined (do not overmix). Cover and refrigerate until serving.

FOR THE COOKIE

Sift together the dry ingredients; place in a mixer with a paddle attachment. Beat in egg whites, scraping sides of bowl. Mix in melted butter and vanilla until just incorporated. Cover and refrigerate until ready to bake.

To form cookies, make a template from a milk carton or 1/16-inch cardboard; using a razor, cut out a 2½-inch x 5-inch rectangle. Place a silpat on the bottom of a baking sheet. Place template on silpat; with an offset spatula, spread the chilled paste flat and even within the template. Carefully remove template and repeat with remaining paste. Bake at 400° for 5 minutes or until lightly browned. While still warm, immediately form each cookie over a box of baking soda to form a rectangular cup.

FOR THE MARSHMALLOW

Line a 13-inch x 9-inch x 2-inch baking pan with parchment and lightly dust with confectioners'

sugar; set aside. In a small bowl, sprinkle gelatin over ¼ cup water; allow to soften. In a saucepan over medium heat, combine sugar, corn syrup, salt and remaining water. Once mixture reaches 230°, begin whipping the egg whites in a mixer on high speed. As soon as the syrup reaches 245°, remove from the heat, lower mixer speed and carefully add syrup to whipping egg whites in a slow, steady stream.

Next add the softened gelatin, making sure it is completely dissolved. Increase mixer speed to high. When meringue has a smooth, light and fluffy consistency, pour into the prepared baking pan. Sift cornstarch over the marshmallow; cool.

Cut marshmallow away from edges of pan and invert onto a cutting board. Peel off parchment and brush off any excess cornstarch. Using a warm, dry knife, cut the marshmallow into 16 pieces (2 inches x 3 inches). Dust with confectioners' sugar to keep them from sticking to each other.

TO PLATE

Lay a sheet of paper over two-thirds of the plate; dust the remaining third of the plate with confectioners' sugar. Fill a squeeze bottle with ganache (see recipe on page 161) and draw a straight line to separate the two sides of the plate. Place cookie on undusted side.

With a wire whisk, whip chocolate mousse to soften. Spoon mousse into cookie cup; top with a marshmallow. Heat Jack Daniels in a small saucepan; once it's on fire, pour over the marshmallow and serve while flaming. If your guests were Scouts, they'll know to blow out their marshmallow before eating. ■

* *Graham Cracker Cookie ingredients need to be measured with a kitchen scale; they will not convert to cups.*

Photo on page 150

BIT-O-HONEY BEEHIVES

Serves 8

FROM THE CHEF ~ This is simply a baked Alaska featuring homemade ice cream made with local honey in place of sugar. Once finished, the dessert appears to be a beehive.

TEXAS HONEY ICE CREAM*

5 egg yolks

2 cups half-and-half cream

1 cup honey

1 cup heavy whipping cream

SPONGECAKE

6 ounces unsalted butter, room temperature

6 ounces granulated sugar, *divided*

6 eggs, room temperature, *separated*

½ teaspoon vanilla extract

½ teaspoon salt

Zest of ½ lemon

4 ounces cake flour

2½ ounces finely ground almonds

10 pieces Bit-o-Honey candy (hand-chopped)

½ cup light corn syrup

12 ounces granulated sugar

½ cup water

1 cup egg whites, room temperature

GARNISH

6 pieces Bit-o-Honey candy

½ cup "151" rum

FOR THE ICE CREAM

In a mixing bowl, whisk egg yolks until fluffy; set aside. In a heavy saucepan, combine half-and-half and honey. Cook and stir over medium-high heat; when mixture comes to a fast simmer, remove from the heat. Slowly whisk 1 cup of warm cream mixture into egg yolks. Whisk this mixture into the saucepan; cook for 1 minute or until the back of a spoon is coated. Remove from the heat; whisk in heavy cream.

Strain into a bowl. Cool to room temperature. Cover and refrigerate overnight. The next day, freeze in an ice cream maker according to the manufacturer's instructions. Transfer to an airtight storage container. Place plastic wrap directly on surface of ice cream. Freeze until firm.

FOR THE SPONGECAKE

In an electric mixer with a paddle attachment, cream the butter with half of the sugar until light and fluffy. Beat in egg yolks, vanilla, salt and lemon zest. In another mixing bowl with a whisk attachment, whip egg whites until frothy; add remaining sugar and whip until soft peaks form. Gently fold egg whites

into egg yolk mixture. Combine the flour, almonds and candy; carefully fold into egg mixture.

Place on a parchment-lined 12-inch x 8-inch pan. Spread batter evenly into pan. Bake at 425° for 10 minutes or until light brown and a toothpick comes out clean. Cool on a wire rack.

FOR THE MERINGUE

In a heavy saucepan, bring corn syrup, sugar and water to a boil. Using a candy thermometer, bring the syrup to 230°. In an electric mixer with a whisk attachment, begin whipping the egg whites on high speed until frothy. Once syrup reaches 240° (soft-ball stage), remove from the heat. Reduce mixer speed to medium; pour syrup in a continuous stream into egg whites. Whip on high until stiff peaks form.

TO ASSEMBLE

Cut spongecake into 3-inch circles. *Work with one cake at a time to keep the ice cream from melting.* Place a scoop of ice cream on each cake circle; reserve in freezer. Place meringue in a pastry bag with a plain tip. Completely cover the ice cream with meringue by piping circles of meringue on top of each other, starting at the bottom and working to the top. Reserve in freezer.

TO PLATE

Place cake on an ovenproof dessert plate; brown lightly with a chef's torch. Sprinkle entire plate with chopped candy. At table side, pour a tablespoon of flaming rum on the cake. ■

* Make ice cream 2 days prior to serving.

CHILLED STRAWBERRY BASIL SOUP

Serves 8

CHAMPAGNE SORBET

1 bottle (750ml) brut sparkling wine

1¼ cups Simple Syrup (recipe
   on page 203)

¾ cup water

3 tablespoons lemon juice

¼ cup finely chopped fresh basil

BASIL OIL

1 cup cottonseed or grapeseed
   oil (flavorless oil)

1 cup packed chiffonade basil

2 tablespoons granulated sugar

SOUP

3 pints fresh strawberries, washed,
   stemmed and quartered

1 cup Simple Syrup (recipe on
   page 203)

1 bottle (750ml) brut sparkling wine

Chiffonade basil for garnish

FROM THE CHEF ~ You'll be surprised how well the licorice flavors of the basil blend with the strawberries. This soup is a light and healthy dessert and more fun than a plate of fruit. It's best prepared the day before serving.

FOR THE SORBET

In a bowl, combine the wine, syrup, water and lemon juice. Freeze in an ice cream maker according to manufacturer's instructions. Transfer to an airtight storage container. Fold in the basil. Freeze.

FOR THE OIL

In a blender, purée the oil, basil and sugar. Refrigerate overnight to allow the basil's chlorophyll to leach into the oil. Strain through a cheesecloth-lined fine mesh strainer. Discard the basil and reserve the green oil; refrigerate.

FOR THE SOUP

In a blender, blend the strawberries and syrup until smooth (blend in batches if necessary). Transfer to a large bowl; stir in the syrup and wine. Strain through a fine mesh strainer; cover and refrigerate.

TO PLATE

Ladle cold soup into large, rimmed, chilled soup bowls. Place a scoop of sorbet in the center; top with a basil. Drizzle a teaspoon of basil oil into the soup for the final garnish. ■

RUSTIC FIG TART WITH VANILLA BEAN CRUST

Serves 6

SUGARCANE-PECAN ICE CREAM*

10 egg yolks

1¼ cups Steen's sugarcane syrup, *divided*

2 cups whole milk

2 cups heavy whipping cream

1 cup pecans, toasted

VANILLA BEAN CRUST

2 cups unsifted all-purpose flour

3 tablespoons granulated sugar

¼ teaspoon salt

1 vanilla bean, split and scraped, seeds reserved

¾ cup cold unsalted butter, cut into small pieces

1 egg yolk

Ice water as needed

FRUIT FILLING

2 cups sliced fresh figs (1 pint)

Juice of ½ lemon

2 tablespoons plus 3 teaspoons granulated sugar, *divided*

3 tablespoons Tokay or other sweet dessert wine

1 egg

1 tablespoon water

FROM THE CHEF ~ Sugarcane is to Louisiana as maple is to Canada. The ice cream is a basic custard recipe, except I replace the sugar with cane syrup. Because of the intense flavor and sweetness of the ice cream, the crust is intentionally not overly sweet. You can make the crust a day ahead.

FOR THE ICE CREAM

In a mixing bowl, whisk egg yolks and ¾ cup syrup until fluffy and pale yellow; set aside. In a heavy saucepan, combine milk, cream and remaining syrup. Cook and stir over medium-high heat; when mixture comes to a fast simmer, remove from the heat. Slowly whisk 1 cup warm cream mixture into egg yolk mixture. Whisk this mixture into the saucepan; cook for 1 minute or until the back of a spoon is coated.

Remove from the heat and strain into a bowl. Cool to room temperature. Cover and refrigerate overnight. The next day, freeze in an ice cream maker according to the manufacturer's instructions. Transfer to an airtight storage container. Fold in toasted pecans. Freeze. ▶

In a large mixing bowl, combine the flour, sugar, salt and vanilla seeds. Cut in butter until mixture resembles coarse crumbs. Add egg yolk. Sprinkle with a small amount of ice water, 1 teaspoon at a time, until dough holds together without being too wet or sticky. (Squeeze a small amount together; if it is crumbly, add more ice water.) Between two sheets of plastic wrap, form dough into a disk and flatten into a 9-inch circle. Refrigerate for at least 30 minutes.

FOR THE FILLING

Remove dough from the refrigerator. In a mixing bowl, gently toss the figs, lemon juice, 2 tablespoons sugar and wine. Marinate for 30 minutes. On a lightly floured surface and using a floured rolling pin, roll out the dough into a large circle, about ¼ inch thick. Using a 6-inch plate, cut six circles from the dough and transfer to a lightly greased baking sheet.

Scoop figs from marinade, reserving marinade. Distribute figs among the tarts, leaving a 2-inch border all around. Beat egg with water; brush over the border. Lift edge of dough over the filling, leaving figs exposed in center. (A rustic tart should be free-form.) Gently fold and pinch the dough to seal any cracks.

Sprinkle 1 teaspoon of reserved marinade over the center of each tart. Brush dough with remaining egg wash; sprinkle with remaining sugar. Bake at 375° for 30 minutes or until crust is golden brown and fruit is bubbly and tender.

TO PLATE

Serve tarts warm or at room temperature with sugarcane-pecan ice cream. ■

* Make the Sugarcane-Pecan Ice Cream 2 days before serving.

BRENNAN'S PEANUT BUTTER CUP

Serves 8

FROM THE CHEF ~ Chocolate and peanut butter have long been a perfect pairing. I decided to take one of my favorite treats and give it my own interpretation.

PEANUT BUTTER ICE CREAM*

10 egg yolks

1¼ cups sugar

2 cups milk

2 cups heavy whipping cream

½ cup creamy peanut butter

PEANUT BRITTLE

¼ cup water

½ cup sugar

¼ cup corn syrup

½ cup salted peanuts, toasted

½ tablespoon butter

Pinch baking soda

CHOCOLATE CUPS*

½ pound bittersweet chocolate

8 foil cupcake liners (2-inch bottom, 1¼-inch sides, 4½-inch circle)

PEANUT BUTTER MOUSSE

1¾ teaspoons unflavored powdered gelatin

2 tablespoons water

1 cup heavy whipping cream

¼ cup confectioners' sugar

1 teaspoon vanilla extract

⅔ cup creamy peanut butter

1 cup milk

PEANUT BUTTER CUSTARD*

½ cup heavy whipping cream

2 tablespoons sugar

¼ cup creamy peanut butter

GANACHE

¼ pound bittersweet chocolate

6 tablespoons heavy whipping cream

FOR THE ICE CREAM

In a mixing bowl, whisk egg yolks and sugar until fluffy; set aside. In a heavy saucepan, combine milk, cream and peanut butter. Cook and stir over medium-high heat; when mixture comes to a fast simmer, remove from the heat. Slowly whisk 1 cup of warm cream mixture into egg yolk mixture. Whisk this mixture into the saucepan; cook for 1 minute or until the back of a spoon is coated.

Remove from the heat and strain into a bowl. (You will need to push the mixture through the strainer since it will be stiff.) Cool to room temperature. Cover and refrigerate overnight. The next day, freeze in an ice cream maker according to the manufacturer's instructions. Transfer to an airtight storage container. Freeze until firm.

FOR THE BRITTLE

In a saucepan, bring water to a boil. Remove from the heat; stir in sugar until dissolved. Stir in corn syrup and return to heat; bring to 250° on a candy thermometer. Remove from the heat; carefully add butter. Cook over low heat until mixture turns medium brown. Gently swirl pan over heat. Do not stir. Mixture will be extremely hot. ▶

Remove from the heat; add the peanuts and baking soda, being careful not to burn yourself. Pour hot brittle onto a silpat-lined pan, scraping out all of the brittle. Spread the molten mixture over the silpat (it will not cover the entire surface). Drag a butter knife through the brittle, making 1-inch squares. Cool; break into pieces and store in an airtight container.

FOR THE CHOCOLATE CUPS

Break or chop chocolate into small pieces. Melt chocolate over a hot-water bath. Dip a pastry brush in melted chocolate and lightly brush a thin layer of chocolate inside cupcake liners. (Keep chocolate warm until you have completed brushing.) Place in a cupcake tin and refrigerate until set. Repeat, adding a second coat of chocolate. Refrigerate until assembling.

FOR THE MOUSSE

In a small bowl, sprinkle gelatin over water; allow to soften. In an electric mixer, whip the cream, confectioners' sugar and vanilla until medium peaks form. In a small saucepan, warm peanut butter and milk, whisking until well combined. Add to the gelatin; strain into a bowl. Fold in the whipped cream mixture. Incorporate completely, but be careful not to overmix.

FOR THE GANACHE

Prepare immediately prior to assembling peanut butter cups. Break or chop chocolate into small pieces; place in a medium heatproof bowl. In a small saucepan over medium heat, bring cream to a boil. Pour over chocolate; let sit for 1 minute so the hot cream begins to melt the chocolate. Slowly stir, starting in center and working to outer edges. Stir until the chocolate is completely melted and all the cream is incorporated.

TO ASSEMBLE

Fill each chocolate cup with ¼ cup of mousse (using a #16 scoop); chill until set. Fill a squeeze bottle with ganache; squeeze over mousse in each cup; chill until set. Set remaining ganache aside for garnish.

FOR THE CUSTARD

In a saucepan over medium-low heat, combine cream and sugar; scald until sugar is dissolved. Place peanut butter in a bowl; whisk in cream mixture until smooth.

TO PLATE

Peel the foil liner from the filled chocolate cups, being careful not to break the hardened chocolate. Place about 2 tablespoons of custard on half of the plate; spread into a 2½-inch circle. Place peanut butter cup on custard. Squeeze a zigzag of ganache on other half of plate. Top with a scoop of ice cream; place three pieces of brittle around ice cream. Finish with a dusting of confectioners' sugar. ■

Make the ice cream 2 days before serving; make the chocolate cups 1 day before serving.

PEACH UPSIDE-DOWN CAKES
Serves 12

FROM THE CHEF ~ We bake these cakes in 4-inch iron blini pans that give a perfect balance between fruit and cake. The best part of any upside-down cake is the caramelized brown sugar crust formed from the edge of the pan. With the mini pans, all edges are caramelized.

1 cup plus 6 tablespoons unsalted butter, softened, *divided*

1¾ cups granulated sugar

3 eggs

1 vanilla bean, split and scraped, seeds reserved

4½ cups cake flour

2 tablespoons baking powder

1 teaspoon salt

1¾ cups milk

1 cup packed light brown sugar

10 to 12 peaches, peeled and sliced

PEACH ICE CREAM*

6 egg yolks

1½ cups granulated sugar, *divided*

3 cups milk

1 cup heavy whipping cream

3 tablespoons peach liqueur

1½ cups peach purée

1½ cups diced peaches

FOR THE ICE CREAM

In a mixing bowl, whisk egg yolks and ¾ cup sugar until fluffy; set aside. In a heavy saucepan, combine milk, cream, liqueur and remaining sugar. Cook and stir over medium-high heat; when mixture comes to a fast simmer, remove from the heat. Slowly whisk half of the warm cream mixture into the egg yolk mixture. Whisk this mixture into the saucepan; cook for 1 minute.

Remove from the heat and strain into a bowl. Stir in the peach purée. Cover and refrigerate overnight. The next day, freeze in an ice cream maker according to the manufacturer's instructions. Fold in diced peaches. Store packed tightly in a covered container. Freeze until firm.

FOR THE CAKES

In an electric mixer with a paddle attachment, cream ½ cup plus 6 tablespoons butter and sugar until light and fluffy. Add eggs, one at a time, beating until combined. Add vanilla seeds. Sift together the flour, baking powder and salt; add to creamed mixture alternately with milk (batter may appear to be curdled).

In 12 small iron skillets, melt the brown sugar and remaining butter until bubbly. Add peaches and remove from the heat. Spoon batter over peaches. Place skillets on baking sheets. Bake at 375° for 25 minutes or until a toothpick comes out clean.

TO PLATE

Let the cakes stand for 5 minutes, then invert onto plates. Top with peach ice cream. ∎

Make the Peach Ice Cream 2 days before serving.

VANILLA BEAN POUND CAKE WITH PRALINE ICE CREAM
Serves 16

CARAMEL SAUCE

2 cups granulated sugar

½ cup water

½ pound unsalted butter, cubed

1⅓ cups heavy whipping cream

PRALINE ICE CREAM*

18 egg yolks

1½ cups granulated sugar

4 cups half-and-half cream

4 cups heavy whipping cream

1 vanilla bean, split and scraped,
  seeds reserved

¼ cup praline liqueur

1 cup medium pecan pieces, toasted

1 recipe Caramel Sauce

POUND CAKE

½ pound unsalted butter, room
  temperature

2 cups granulated sugar

1½ vanilla beans, split and scraped,
  seeds reserved

7 eggs, room temperature

2 cups unsifted all-purpose flour

Pinch salt

FROM THE CHEF ~ Nothing says "home" like my mother's pound cake. She always had one in the kitchen ready for us to snack on. I think it is a must to have this dessert at the Kitchen Table as part of my "home away from home."

FOR THE SAUCE

In a heavy saucepan, heat the sugar and water over medium-high heat. Carefully swirl the pan over the heat until sugar is dissolved. Increase heat to high and boil the syrup until the edges begin to brown. Do not stir. Again carefully swirl the pan until the syrup turns an amber color. Remove from the heat; being extremely cautious, stir in the butter until combined. Then stir in the cream. Store covered at room temperature.

FOR THE ICE CREAM

In a mixing bowl, whisk egg yolks and sugar until fluffy; set aside. In a heavy saucepan, combine half-and-half, heavy cream and vanilla seeds. Cook and stir over medium-high heat; when mixture comes to a fast simmer, remove from the heat. Slowly whisk 1 cup of warm cream mixture into egg yolk mixture. Whisk this mixture into the saucepan; cook for 1 minute.

Remove from the heat and strain into a bowl. Stir in the praline liqueur. Cool, then ▶

cover and refrigerate overnight. The next day, freeze in an ice cream maker according to the manufacturer's instructions.

Place 2 cups of ice cream in a storage container; top with ¼ cup toasted pecans and drizzle with ½ cup caramel sauce. Marblelize with a knife. Repeat the layers three times. Place in an airtight container. Freeze. Reserve remaining caramel sauce for garnishing.

FOR THE POUND CAKE

In an electric mixer with a paddle attachment, cream butter and sugar for 10 minutes or until fluffy, scraping the sides of the bowl. Add vanilla seeds. On low speed, beat in the eggs, one at a time. Combine flour and salt; add to creamed mixture a third at a time, scraping sides of bowl after each addition. Only mix until incorporated.

Pour into two 8-inch x 4-inch x 3-inch loaf pans coated with nonstick cooking spray. Bake at 325° for 1¼ hours or until a toothpick comes out clean. Cool for 10 minutes before removing from pans to a wire rack to cool completely.

TO PLATE

Cut each loaf into eight equal slices. Melt 2 tablespoons butter in a sauté pan over medium heat. Brown cake slices on both sides until golden. Drizzle 1 tablespoon of praline liqueur on each slice. Remove from pan and cut the slice in half on a bias. On each plate, place one half cake piece standing on its side and the other lying flat next to it. Top with a scoop of ice cream; drizzle reserved caramel sauce around the cake. Serve while cake is still warm. ■

Make the Praline Ice Cream 2 days before serving.

Meyer Lemon Mini Spice Cakes

Serves 18

3 cups all-purpose flour

3 cups packed dark brown sugar

1 tablespoon cinnamon

1 teaspoon nutmeg

1 tablespoon baking soda

1¾ cups vegetable oil

6 eggs

1 vanilla bean, split and scraped, seeds reserved

1 teaspoon lemon extract

3 tablespoons Meyer lemon zest

MEYER LEMON SHERBET

2 cups water

2 cups granulated sugar

2 cups sour cream

3 cups Meyer lemon juice

CANDIED CITRUS ZEST

¼ cup water

1 cup granulated sugar, *divided*

½ cup finely julienned Meyer lemon zest

FROM THE CHEF ~ Meyer lemons grow well on the Gulf Coast. We buy ours from Froberg Farms in Alvin, Texas. Meyers are so sweet you can eat them like an orange! If you do not have Meyers, you can us any other citrus available. I also like to use Froberg's satsuma oranges, which are similar to a honey tangerine.

Instead of jumbo muffin cups, you can bake these cakes in mini Bundt pans or one 12-inch Bundt pan. For the candied zest, you can use oranges or limes or a combination of citrus.

FOR THE SHERBET

In a saucepan, bring water and sugar to a boil. Cool slightly, then whisk in the sour cream and lemon juice. Refrigerate until chilled. Freeze in an ice cream maker according to manufacturer's instructions.

FOR THE CAKES

In a large bowl, stir by hand the flour, brown sugar, cinnamon, nutmeg and baking soda. Add oil, eggs, vanilla seeds, lemon extract and zest; slowly stir until batter is smooth. Pour 2⅔ ounces (#12 scoop) into well-greased jumbo (4-inch) muffin cups. Bake at 375° for 20-25 minutes or until a toothpick comes out clean. Cool for 10 minutes before removing from pans to wire racks.

FOR THE CANDIED ZEST

In a small saucepan over high heat, bring water, ¼ cup sugar and zest to a boil. Boil for 7 minutes, stirring often so the zest doesn't burn. Place remaining sugar in a pie pan. Using a fork place zest into sugar; turn to coat. Place on a paper-lined pan to dry.

TO PLATE

Place mini cakes in the center of each plate; top with a scoop of sherbet and a crown of candied zest. ∎

POPCORN RICE CRÈME CARAMEL

Serves 10

LOUISIANA POPCORN RICE

1½ cups water

½ teaspoon salt

½ cup popcorn rice or other
   aromatic rice

CRÈME CARAMEL*

1 cup granulated sugar

½ teaspoon lemon juice

4 eggs

4 egg yolks

2¼ cups whole milk

2 cans cream of coconut
   (Coco Lopez)

¼ cup sugar

1 vanilla bean, split and scraped,
   seeds reserved

1 teaspoon ground cinnamon

1½ cups cooked Louisiana
   Popcorn Rice

COCONUT TUILE BATTER*

6 tablespoons unsalted butter,
   softened, cubed

1½ cups flaked coconut

¾ cup granulated sugar

3 tablespoons milk

2 tablespoons cake flour

Vegetable oil

½ cup Rice Krispies

RUM RAISINS*

½ cup golden raisins

½ cup raisins

½ cup rum

FROM THE CHEF ~ I have always
loved arroz con leche and flan
— two South Texas favorites.
This dessert is a combination
of the two.

FOR THE RICE

In a saucepan, bring water and salt to a boil. Add rice.
Cover and reduce the heat; simmer for 20 minutes or
until rice is tender and water is absorbed.

FOR THE CRÈME CARAMEL

In a heavy saucepan, melt sugar. Stir in lemon juice
and watch for the sugar to start turning a golden brown
color, swirling the pan gently over the heat. Remove
from the heat. Distribute evenly among ten 6-ounce
ceramic ramekins; set aside.

In a mixing bowl, whisk the eggs and yolks; set aside.
In another heavy saucepan, scald the milk, cream of
coconut, sugar, vanilla bean and cinnamon. Remove
from the heat. Slowly whisk 1 cup of warm milk mixture
into egg mixture in a thin stream. Pour egg mixture into
milk mixture while continuing to whisk. Cook over a
hot-water bath for 30 minutes or until custard reaches
the consistency of lemon curd. ▶

Pour custard into ramekins, filling half full. Place 2 tablespoons cooked rice in the middle of each ramekin; top off with more custard. Place in a large baking pan; add hot water to pan until it's halfway up the sides of ramekins. Cover pan with plastic wrap and then foil. Bake at 300° for 1½ hours or until set. Cool; chill overnight.

Dip custards in a bowl of warm water to loosen; invert onto plate. Place a spoonful of raisins at the base of custard and garnish with coconut tuile. ■

Make the crème caramel 1 day prior to serving. The tuile batter and rum raisins may be made a day ahead.

FOR THE TUILE BATTER

In a food processor, cream butter until fluffy. Add coconut and sugar; blend until well combined, scraping sides of bowl. Slowly blend in milk. Add flour and blend for 5 minutes. Remove from processor and refrigerate until firm, about 1½ hours.

Liberally grease a parchment-lined jelly-roll pan with vegetable oil. With oiled fingertips, place a tablespoon of tuile batter on the pan and spread with your hands into a circle about 4 inches in diameter ⅛ inch thick (until you can see a hint of the parchment; they will spread upon baking). Sprinkle each disk with Rice Krispies.

Bake at 375° for 7 minutes or until golden brown. Cool for about 15 seconds. Cut tuiles into 3-inch disks with a 3-inch metal ring dipped in oil after each use. Remove tuiles to a parchment-lined baking sheet to cool. Store in an airtight container for up to 2 days before using.

FOR THE RAISINS

Combine the ingredients in a small saucepan. Bring to a simmer over medium heat; cook for about 10 minutes or until raisins have absorbed all the rum but aren't dry.

CREOLE CREAM CHEESE CRÊPES WITH TEXAS STRAWBERRIES
Serves 4

FROM THE CHEF ~ Creole Cream Cheese is simply a fresh cow's milk cheese that New Orleanians like to eat with fresh berries or use to make ice cream or cheesecake.

CREOLE CREAM CHEESE*

½ gallon whole milk

¼ rennet tab

¼ cup buttermilk

¼ cup granulated sugar, reserved

SWEETENED CRÈME FRAÎCHE*

¼ cup heavy whipping cream

1 tablespoon buttermilk

1 tablespoon granulated sugar, reserved

SWEET CRÊPES

¾ cup unsifted all-purpose flour

½ tablespoon granulated sugar

Pinch salt

1 cup milk

3 eggs, lightly beaten

1 teaspoon vanilla extract

2 tablespoons butter, cubed

1/3 cup granulated sugar

1 cup halved fresh strawberries

GARNISH

12 fresh strawberries, quartered

3 tablespoons chiffonade mint

FOR THE CREAM CHEESE

Heat the milk to 80°-90°. (It is very important not to add rennet if milk is hotter. Like yeast, rennet is heat-sensitive; it will die if the milk is over 90°.) Crush the rennet tab into pieces. Add buttermilk and rennet to warm milk. Pour into a rectangular baking dish or shallow pan with sides tall enough to hold mixture. Cover with cheesecloth and let stand at room temperature overnight.

The next day, place a cheesecloth-lined colander over a pan. (Fold cheesecloth a few times to make it stronger.) Drain cheese through the cheesecloth. Place in the refrigerator for 24 hours while it drains into the pan. Save the curds on the cheesecloth; drain and discard whey in the pan.

FOR THE CRÈME FRAÎCHE

Combine cream and buttermilk in a nonreactive container. Cover with cheesecloth; let stand at room temperature overnight. The next day, place mixture in refrigerator overnight to thicken. Prior to using, transfer to a mixing bowl and whip in sugar. Refrigerate until needed.

FOR THE CRÊPES

In a medium bowl, combine flour, sugar and salt. Combine the milk, eggs and vanilla; add to dry ingredients and whisk until smooth. Strain batter through a fine mesh strainer; refrigerate for at least 30 minutes.

Coat an 8-inch nonstick skillet with sloped sides with nonstick cooking spray; heat over medium-high heat. Pour 2 tablespoons batter into skillet; rotate and tilt pan to distribute evenly, covering entire bottom of pan but not sides. Cook for 1 minute or until golden and set; flip and cook other side until lightly golden. Repeat until all crêpes are made. Stack between sheets of waxed paper. Serve immediately, refrigerate until needed, or tightly wrap and freeze for up to 1 month.

FOR THE SAUCE

Melt butter in a small sauté pan over medium heat; add sugar and strawberries. Cook for 3-4 minutes or until strawberries are soft and syrup has formed. Remove from the heat; purée until smooth. Keep warm.

TO PLATE

In a mixing bowl, whisk Creole cream cheese to thicken. Mix in ¼ cup sugar. Transfer to a pastry bag. Fold crêpes in half, then in half again to form a triangle; place in center of plate with tips pointing in. Pipe cream cheese into folded crêpes. Pour strawberry sauce around and over crêpes. Place a dollop of crème fraîche in center of crêpes. Arrange quartered strawberries around the plate and top with mint. ■

* Allow 3 days to prepare the Creole Cream Cheese. Or you may purchase it from Bittersweet Plantation (see information on page 147). Allow 2 days to prepare the Sweetened Crème Fraîche.

OPEN KITCHEN — Since every party ends up in the kitchen, we start ours here!

On Wednesday nights in June and July, our guests have a chance to meet our chefs, learn from winemakers, visit with farmers and ranchers plus see cooking demonstrations — all in the kitchen. There's no RSVP needed, and everything is on the house. That means less work for us and more fun. Open Kitchen Nights are our chance to relax and enjoy.

In this chapter we've included some of the cocktails and hors d'oeuvres that have been popular at this event. I invite you to give them a try and open your kitchen to friends and family.

BRANDY CRUSTA

WATERMELON MARGARITAS

MILK AND COOKIES

MINT JULEP MODERNE

POMEGRANATE DAIQUIRI

CREOLE MARTINI WITH
CRAB-STUFFED OLIVES

CABRITO LOLLIPOPS

SNO-CONES

VENISON REUBENS

DUCK CONFIT POPPERS

freeze until serving. Purée the macerated pulp in a blender. Strain through a fine mesh strainer; reserve juice for margaritas.

Combine the watermelon juice, tequila, syrup and key lime juice in a shaker; shake vigorously. Strain into a salt- and sugar-rimmed glass filled with ice. Garnish with limes and frozen drunken melon balls. ∎

DRUNKEN WATERMELON MARGARITA

Serves 1

DRUNKEN WATERMELON

1 watermelon (20 pounds)

1 bottle añejo tequila

WATERMELON MARGARITA

¼ cup watermelon juice

1 ¼ ounces añejo tequila (shot)

¼ ounce Simple Syrup (recipe on page 203)

Juice of 1 key lime

Limes for garnish

Cut a small hole in the watermelon; place tequila bottle into the hole and refrigerate overnight. The next day, using a parisienne scoop (melon baller), make balls from the melon (three per glass) and

BRANDY CRUSTA

Serves 1

FROM THE CHEF ~ Joe Santini invented the Crusta in *Daily Lush*'s hometown of New Orleans. What makes it a Crusta is sugar on the rim of the glass. This drink has an interesting genealogy: The Crusta is father to the sidecar cocktail and grandfather to the margarita. This is our version of this classic drink.

1 ounce brandy VSOP

½ ounce Grand Marnier

¼ ounce maraschino liqueur

¼ ounce Simple Syrup (recipe on page 203)

¼ ounce Cointreau

Juice of 1 lemon

Dash Grenadine

Combine all ingredients with ice in a shaker; shake well. Serve in a sugar-rimmed flute. ∎

Photo on next page

open kitchen

Milk and Cookies

FROM THE CHEF ~ I had this idea one Christmas Eve to serve milk (actually, brandy milk punch) and cookies to the adults at every table at the end of the meal. People still tell me how much fun that was for them. I figure you're never too old for "milk and cookies" before Santa shows up!

We use a scoop to shape uniform 1-inch balls of the cookie dough. Crushed molasses sugar cookies make a great crust for pumpkin cheesecake or a garnish for coffee ice cream.

Molasses Sugar Cookies
Makes 4 dozen

¾ cup vegetable oil

¼ cup molasses

1 teaspoon vanilla extract

1 egg

1½ cups sugar, *divided*

2 cups all-purpose flour

2 teaspoons baking soda

½ teaspoon salt

1½ teaspoons ground cinnamon

½ teaspoon ground cloves

Brandy Milk Punch
Serves 1

1½ ounces brandy

½ ounce vanilla extract

½ ounce Simple Syrup (recipe on page 203)

2 ounces milk

1 ounce half-and-half cream

Sprinkle of grated nutmeg

FOR THE COOKIES

In an electric mixer with a paddle attachment, combine the oil, molasses, vanilla, egg and 1 cup sugar. Sift together the flour, baking soda, salt, cinnamon and cloves; add to molasses mixture and mix well. Cover dough with plastic wrap and chill for at least 3 hours or overnight.

Place the remaining sugar in a shallow bowl. Form 1-inch balls of dough and roll in sugar. Place 2 inches apart on parchment-lined baking sheets. Bake at 375° for 8-10 minutes (do not overbake). Cookies will appear soft but will set up after cooling. Cool for 5 minutes before removing to wire racks. Serve warm or store in an airtight container until serving.

FOR THE MILK PUNCH

In an ice-filled shaker, combine the brandy, vanilla, syrup, milk and cream; shake well. Strain into glass. Garnish with nutmeg.

TO PLATE

Serve warm cookies with a frosty glass of milk punch. ∎

MINT JULEP MODERNE

Serves 1

3 ounces aged bourbon

3 ounces mint tea

Mint leaves for garnish

MINT TEA

Makes 2 cups

2 cups water

¾ cup granulated sugar

2 cups packed fresh mint leaves

FOR THE TEA

In a small saucepan, bring water to a boil. Place
the sugar in a heatproof container; pour water over
sugar and stir until dissolved. Pack mint into the
sugar water and press with a plate to submerge the
mint below the water. Cover and let sit overnight.
Strain and reserve.

TO SERVE

Combine the bourbon and tea in a shaker. Fill
with ice and shake well. Strain into a martini
glass; garnish with a mint leaf. Serve before
the ice crystals melt. ■

POMEGRANATE DAIQUIRI

Serves 1

½ lime, quartered

½ ounce Simple Syrup (recipe on page 203)

1½ ounces pomegranate juice

1½ ounces aged rum

Place the lime in a shaker and muddle. Add the
syrup, pomegranate juice and rum. Fill with
ice and shake well. Strain into a sugar-rimmed
martini glass; serve immediately before the ice
crystals melt. ■

1 ½ ounces tomato juice

1 ½ ounces Absolut Peppar vodka

½ ounce vermouth

½ ounce Worcestershire sauce

2 teaspoons beef broth

¼ teaspoon oyster sauce

Pinch celery salt

Dash Tabasco

Dash Srichaca Hot Chili Sauce

Freshly ground black pepper to taste

CRAB-STUFFED OLIVES

½ cup lump crabmeat

1 teaspoon Creole Seafood Seasoning (recipe
   on page 198)

18 cocktail olives

1 egg

½ cup milk

1 cup breadcrumbs

1 cup all-purpose flour

Salt and black pepper to taste

6 cups vegetable oil (for frying)

FOR THE OLIVES

Season the crab with seafood seasoning; stuff into
the olives. In a shallow bowl, beat the egg and
milk. Season breadcrumbs and flour with salt and
pepper. Bread olives in flour, dip with egg wash and
coat with breadcrumbs. Heat oil to 365°; fry olives
until golden brown. Place on a towel-lined plate.

FOR THE MARTINI

Place the ingredients in a shaker filled with ice
and shake well. Rim a martini glass with salt
and pepper; strain martini into glass. Serve three
crab-stuffed olives on the side. ■

CREOLE MARTINI WITH CRAB-STUFFED OLIVES

Serves 1

FROM THE CHEF ~ The first time we served
this drink with the crab-stuffed olives was for
a fund-raiser. Everyone who had one asked for
a second, and I knew it was a fun combination.

PECAN-CRUSTED CABRITO LOLLIPOPS

Serves 16

2 cabrito racks, frenched (8 bones
    and about 1 ½ pounds *each*)
2 tablespoons Creole Meat Seasoning
    (recipe on page 198)
¼ cup Satsuma Marmalade (recipe
    on page 82)

2 cups Spiced Pecans (recipe on
    page 199), *divided*
¼ cup dried breadcrumbs
¼ cup vegetable oil

CREOLE MUSTARD-ORANGE
GASTRIQUE

¼ cup Satsuma Marmalade (recipe
    on page 82)
¼ cup Creole mustard
1 tablespoon cider vinegar
½ teaspoon red pepper flakes
Salt to taste

FROM THE CHEF ~ Cabrito is
young, suckling goat. If that's
not available, you can use petite
veal racks instead.

FOR THE CABRITO

Rub the cabrito with meat seasoning and then with
marmalade. Pulse 1 cup pecans in a food processor
until mixture is fine, but not oily; blend in breadcrumbs.
Roll the racks in the pecan meal until encrusted. Cover
exposed bones with foil. Heat oil in a large sauté pan
over medium-high heat; sear the racks for 2 minutes on
each side, being cautious not to burn the pecans. Roast
at 400° for 10 minutes or until internal temperature
reaches 120°. Remove from the oven and allow to rest
for 5 minutes.

FOR THE GASTRIQUE

In a small saucepan, heat the marmalade and mustard.
Once the mixture comes to a simmer, whisk in the
vinegar, pepper flakes and salt; bring to a boil. Remove
from the heat and keep warm.

TO PLATE

Sprinkle the remaining spiced pecans over a serving
platter; place a small ramekin of gastrique in the center.
Slice the racks into small chops (lollipops); arrange
around the platter with the bones facing out. ■

SNO-CONES

FROM THE CHEF ~ The sno-cone idea came about one summer when a sno-cone shop opened near my house ... a sno-cone fanatic as a kid, I had to have one. The same day, we were planning a summer cooking class and thought it would be fun to make adult sno-cones.

The Blueberry Meyer Lemon sno-cone was our first creation. Texas blueberries were in season at the time, and I love blueberries with lemon, so it just seemed like a perfect fit. Everyone in the class, which is held in the kitchen, loved them, so we decided to do a few others for our annual Mardi Gras party.

BLUEBERRY MEYER LEMON MARTINI

2 pints blueberries
¼ cup sugar
2 tablespoons lemon juice
Charbay Meyer Lemon vodka

FOR THE BLUEBERRY SYRUP
In a small saucepan over medium heat, cook the blueberries, sugar and lemon juice for 5-10 minutes or until berries are soft, tender and syrupy. Remove from the heat; purée in a blender and strain through a fine mesh strainer. Use a 1:1 ratio of blueberry syrup to vodka.

MANGO MOJITO
6 mint leaves
¼ ounce mango syrup
1 ounce mango purée
1½ ounces Southern Comfort
Juice of 1 lemon

MARDI GRAS HURRICANE

¾ lime, quartered and muddled

¾ ounce Simple Syrup (recipe on page 203)

1 ounce passion fruit syrup

1 ounce cranberry juice

1 ounce aged rum

1 ounce dark rum

¾ ounce sloe gin

½ ounce Campari

shaved ice. Pack a funnel or a ladle that is the same diameter as the martini glass with shaved ice; pour remaining drink over the ice. Serve with a straw and any appropriate garnish. ∎

FOR THE SNO-CONES

Fill a shaker with ice; add the Blueberry Meyer Lemon Martini, Mango Mojito or Mardi Gras Hurricane ingredients. Shake well. Strain half of the cocktail over a martini glass filled with

OPEN-FACED VENISON REUBENS

Serves 8

4 slices marbled rye bread,
    ½-inch slices

2 tablespoons butter, melted

1½ pounds thinly sliced venison
    pastrami

4 ounces thinly sliced Grùyere

4 teaspoons Russian Dressing

1 recipe Fennel Sauerkraut

½ ounce micro red mustard greens

½ cup cider vinegar

1 teaspoon pickling spices

1 teaspoon sugar

¼ teaspoon salt

1 bulb fennel

6 tablespoons mayonnaise

2 tablespoons chili sauce

½ tablespoon sour cream

1 teaspoon minced yellow onion

1 teaspoon dill pickle relish

½ teaspoon chopped parsley

⅛ teaspoon lemon juice

Dash Tabasco

Salt and black pepper to taste

FROM THE CHEF ~ This makes for an outstanding hors d'oeurve. I like to use venison pastrami, particularly from Broken Arrow Ranch, but traditional corned beef or even tasso ham can be used.

FOR THE SAUERKRAUT

In a small saucepan, heat the vinegar, pickling spices, sugar and salt over high heat. With a mandoline, shave the bulb of the fennel into a nonreactive container. Once the vinegar mixture has come to a boil, strain it into the container over the fennel. Refrigerate until cooled, about 1 hour.

FOR THE DRESSING

Combine all of the ingredients in a small mixing bowl; adjust seasoning. Refrigerate until serving.

TO PLATE

Cut the rye into rounds using a 1½-inch ring cutter. Dip both sides in melted butter and sear in a sauté pan over medium heat for 2 minutes on each side. Place the rounds on a baking sheet. Top with 1 ounce of pastrami, 1 tablespoon of sauerkraut and ½ ounce of cheese. Broil until cheese is melted and bubbly. Top with ½ teaspoon of dressing and micro greens. Place on a small plate. ∎

just because we can!

DUCK CONFIT POPPERS
Makes 20

20 hot cherry peppers, roasted,
    skinned and seeded

1 egg

½ cup milk

1½ cups all-purpose flour

1½ cups breadcrumbs

Salt and black pepper to taste

6 cups vegetable oil (for frying)

1 tablespoon vegetable oil

¼ cup finely chopped yellow onion

¼ cup finely chopped poblano chile

¼ cup finely chopped red bell pepper

1 teaspoon minced garlic

1 recipe Duck Confit (recipe on
    page 200), shredded

1 tablespoon Louisiana hot sauce

1 tablespoon Worcestershire sauce

½ cup shredded jalapeño cheese

1 cup mayonnaise

¼ cup sour cream

¼ cup white vinegar

1 tablespoon minced shallots

1 teaspoon minced garlic

1 tablespoon minced fresh cilantro

Salt and black pepper to taste

FROM THE CHEF ~ Attention, Chile Heads! Pick your pepper, and make this dish as hot as you like it. I use hot cherry peppers that are off the Scoville scale.

FOR THE CONFIT MIX

Heat oil in a medium sauté pan over medium-high heat; sauté the onion, poblano, bell pepper and garlic until onion is translucent. Add duck, hot sauce and Worcestershire sauce; heat through. Add cheese and heat until melted. Season with salt and pepper. Cool.

FOR THE DRESSING

In a small bowl, combine the mayonnaise, sour cream, vinegar, shallots, garlic and cilantro. Season with salt and pepper. Store in the refrigerator for up to 5 days.

TO PLATE

Cut off the tip of each pepper, leaving stem attached (to use as a handle if passed as an hors d'ouerve). Stuff the peppers with cooled confit mix. In a small bowl, beat egg and milk. Roll peppers in flour, dredge in egg wash and dust with breadcrumbs seasoned with salt and pepper. Heat oil in a fryer to 365°; fry peppers until golden brown. Drain on a towel-lined plate. Serve on a platter with cilantro dressing. ■

the pantry

Tricks | Terms | Techniques

This chapter is a compilation of recipes that are basic to the repertoire in most kitchens, along with some recipes we use in multiple dishes in this book. From seasoning blends to stocks, we use these recipes to add life to the finished dishes. The key is to start with quality ingredients to yield incredible dishes.

(fig. 1)

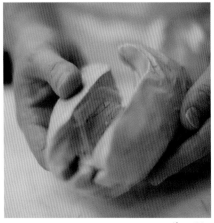
(fig. 2)

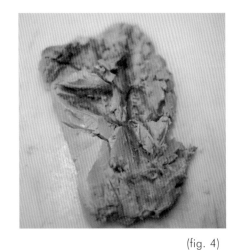
(fig. 3)

(fig. 4)

(fig. 5)

(fig. 6)

Cleaning Foie Gras

After soaking foie gras overnight, remove from the milk.

Let stand, covered, at room temperature for 20 minutes. (fig.1)

Separate foie gras into its two lobes. (fig. 2)

With a paring knife, carefully remove the thin transparent membrane surrounding the surface of the liver. (fig. 3)

Carefully dissect the lobe bilaterally with the tip of a paring knife.

Location of veins prior to removal. (fig. 4)

Extricate veins, with the bottom side up, by following the vein that starts at the narrow end and runs the length of the liver. (fig. 5)

Season foie gras. Sandwich the lobes together, putting posterior and anterior ends together.

Roll foie gras tightly in a 2-foot x 2-foot sheet of plastic wrap. Twist ends in opposite directions to tighten the cylinder. Refrigerate overnight. (fig. 6)

Prepping the Soft-Shell Crab

Remove the eyes from the head. (fig. 1)

Remove gills from under both sides of head. (fig. 2)

Remove the tail from the body.

Squeeze the innards through the eye sockets, being careful not to pull off the dangling legs. (fig. 3)

Stuff the head with seasoned and dressed jumbo lump crabmeat. (fig. 4)

Dredge crab in seasoned flour. Dip into egg wash. Dredge in peanut meal. (fig. 5)

Lay soft-shell on a metal spoon, with legs straddling the handle. (fig. 6)

Carefully fry legs in hot oil for 1 minute, then turn the body over in the oil with legs facing up. Continue frying for 3-5 minutes until golden brown and cook through.

(fig. 1)

(fig. 2)

(fig. 3)

(fig. 4)

(fig. 5)

(fig. 6)

Techniques

Brunoise – small dice, ⅛ inch; items are first julienned, then cut crosswise

Chiffonade – thin strips or shreds of leafy vegetables or herbs

Concassé – tomatoes that have been peeled, seeded and chopped

Deglaze – to dissolve food particles and caramelized drippings left in a pan after roasting or sautéing

Emulsify – to slowly add one ingredient to another while at the same time mixing rapidly

Flambé – to sprinkle food with liquor and ignite to enhance the flavor. Caution: never pour liquor directly from the bottle into the hot pan.

Fond – the concentrated juices, drippings and bits of food left in pans after roasting or sautéing; it is used to flavor sauces made directly in the pans in which the foods were cooked

French – to cut the meat away from the end of a rib or chop so that part of the bone is exposed

Julienne – to cut into ⅛-inch matchsticks

Milk corn – to scrape cob to release the milk after removing kernels

Roast pepper – Rub pepper with olive oil. Roast over an open flame, charring on all sides. Place in a bowl; cover and let stand for 5-10 minutes. Peel skin.

Sweat – to cook in a small amount of fat over low heat until translucent

Terms

Mandoline – slicing device of stainless steel with carbon-steel blades

Mirliton or Chayote – resembles a large pale green pear, found in most Hispanic or Asian markets

Ramp – wild onion that resembles a scallion with broad leaves, also known as a wild leek, found at farmers markets in the spring

Silpat – nonstick silicone liner for baking pans, www.surlatable.com

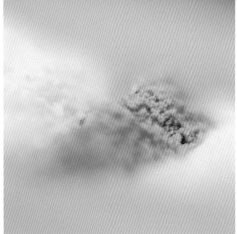

The Art and Science of Seasoning

The most important process of any cooking technique is seasoning, yet it's also the most overlooked. Listen to your taste buds; they know when there isn't enough seasoning. All four basic tastes — salt, sweet, sour and bitter — must be taken into consideration when cooking.

First and foremost is salt. It has been vilified when used heavily, but when applied with a skilled hand, it will perform miracles. Salt is tasted near the front sides of the tongue. For everyday cooking, we use kosher salt, which has been processed very little and is quite pure. The additives in traditional table salt interfere with your taste buds, giving food an off-flavor. Sea salt is excellent when finishing a dish once it has been removed from the heat; it adds minerality.

The sense of sweetness, whether from added sugar or from the natural sweetness of the ingredients, is an integral part of seasoning. Sugars are tasted at the tip of the tongue, hence immediate gratification from sweets such as candy.

Sour flavors make your mouth water and provide crispness necessary to make food seem less heavy, especially fatty dishes. Acids or sour foods — such as vinegar, wine or citrus — are sensed near the back of your tongue. Acids make you salivate, which causes the urge to take another bite. Everyone has eaten a sour pickle and winced, but then gone back for that second bite.

Bitter is a taste that alone is unwanted, but paired with the other three sensations, is welcomed. Bitter is sensed in the throat or thought of as an aftertaste. Caramelized sugars or bitter greens like frisée give dishes the necessary hint of bitterness needed to balance the senses.

Balance is the key to seasoning ... the taste buds must sense salty, sweet, sour and bitter to give a dish complexity. Food can seem flat or one-dimensional without these essential components. If one is missing, the others may seem overly present; however, with the addition of the missing flavor, harmony is achieved.

Some of these flavors come naturally in the food, but others may need to be added. Taste throughout the cooking process and season as you go ... it will add depth and character to your recipe.

Creole Seafood Seasoning

Makes 1¹⁄₃ cups

½ cup salt

¼ cup plus 2 tablespoons paprika

2 tablespoons plus ½ teaspoon
   granulated onion

2 tablespoons plus 1 teaspoon dried thyme

2 tablespoons granulated garlic

2 tablespoons finely ground black pepper

4 teaspoons dried oregano

2½ teaspoons cayenne pepper

In a food processor or bowl, mix all ingredients until thoroughly combined. Cover and store in a cool, dry place.

☙

Creole Meat Seasoning

Makes 1½ cups

½ cup salt

¼ cup plus 2 tablespoons paprika

3 tablespoons granulated garlic

2 tablespoons plus ½ teaspoon
   granulated onion

2 tablespoons finely ground black pepper

2½ teaspoons cayenne pepper

In a food processor or bowl, mix all ingredients until thoroughly combined. Cover and store in a cool, dry place.

☙

Ravigote Sauce

Makes 2½ cups

1½ cups mayonnaise

²⁄₃ cup Creole mustard

1 hard-cooked egg, chopped

2 tablespoons chopped capers

1 tablespoon chopped fresh herbs
   (basil, thyme or oregano)

1 tablespoon Louisiana hot sauce

1 tablespoon Worcestershire sauce

Salt and black pepper to taste

In a bowl, combine the mayonnaise, mustard, egg, capers, herbs, hot sauce and Worcestershire sauce; blend well. Season with salt and pepper. Store in a covered container in the refrigerator for up to 5 days.

☙

Rémoulade Sauce

Makes 1¼ cups

¼ cup finely chopped green onions

2 tablespoons finely chopped celery

2 tablespoons finely chopped parsley

2 tablespoons ketchup

2 tablespoons prepared horseradish

2 tablespoons Creole mustard

1 tablespoon prepared yellow mustard

1 tablespoon white vinegar

2 teaspoons lemon juice

¾ teaspoon paprika

1 egg

1 clove garlic, minced

⅛ teaspoon salt

Pinch cayenne pepper

Dash Tabasco

6 tablespoons vegetable oil

Place the first 15 ingredients in a blender or food processor; mix at high speed until well blended. While processing, gradually add the oil in a slow, steady stream. Sauce will thicken to a creamy consistency. Store in a covered container in the refrigerator for up to 1 week.

☙

Creole Tomato Sauce

Makes 4 cups

2 tablespoons vegetable oil

1 cup chopped onion

1 cup chopped green bell pepper

1 cup chopped celery

2 cloves garlic, minced

2 cups tomato concassé

¼ cup tomato paste

1 cup Shrimp Stock (recipe on page 202)
   or water

4 teaspoons Worcestershire sauce

4 teaspoons Louisiana hot sauce

1½ tablespoons Creole Seafood
   Seasoning (recipe on page 198)

1½ tablespoons cornstarch

½ cup cold water

¼ cup sliced green onions

2 tablespoons chopped fresh herbs
   (basil, thyme *and/or* oregano)

Heat oil in a large saucepan over medium-high heat. Sauté the onion, bell pepper, celery and garlic until onion is translucent. Stir in tomato concassé and paste; cook for 3 minutes. Add stock, Worcestershire sauce, hot sauce and seafood seasoning; bring to a boil. In a small bowl, mix cornstarch and cold water; stir into sauce and return to a boil. Remove from the heat; add green onions and herbs.

⋈

Seafood Boil

Makes about 1 quart

1 quart water

Juice of 1 lemon

¼ cup coarsely chopped celery

¼ cup coarsely chopped carrot

¼ cup coarsely chopped onion

5 teaspoons liquid crab boil

3 teaspoons salt

2 bay leaves

1½ teaspoons Louisiana hot sauce

1½ teaspoons Worcestershire sauce

1½ teaspoons Creole Seafood Seasoning
   (recipe on page 198)

1½ teaspoons black peppercorns

1 teaspoon cayenne pepper

½ teaspoon minced garlic

In a large saucepan, combine all ingredients. Bring to a boil; reduce heat and simmer for 5 minutes. Don't let liquid reduce too much or you may throw off the seasoning. Taste; the boil should taste a little salty.

⋈

Spiced Peanuts

Makes 2 cups

2 cups peanuts

2 tablespoons Creole Seafood Seasoning
   (recipe on page 198)

2 tablespoons Louisiana hot sauce

2 tablespoons Worcestershire sauce

Mix all ingredients in a medium bowl. Spread on a baking sheet. Roast at 350° for 30-45 minutes, stirring every 15 minutes, or until dry and crispy. Cool to room temperature. Store in a covered container.

For Spiced Pecans

Makes 2 cups

Prepare recipe as directed, using 2 cups of coarsely chopped pecans.

⋈

Olive Tapenade

Makes 1 cup

1 tablespoon olive oil
¼ cup brunoise yellow onion
½ tablespoon minced garlic
1 brunoise roasted red bell pepper
1 tablespoon minced anchovies
1 tablespoon minced capers
¼ cup brunoise black olives, pitted
2 tablespoons toasted sliced almonds
½ tablespoon herbes de Provence
2 tablespoons red wine vinegar
Salt to taste

Heat oil over medium heat in a small
sauté pan; sweat the onion and garlic for
3 minutes. Remove from the heat; add bell
pepper, anchovies, capers, olives, almonds
and herbs. Stir in the vinegar, ½ tablespoon
at a time, until the desired consistency and
flavor is reached. Place in a small container
to cool. Adjust seasoning to taste.

ᛐ

Wild Mushroom Ragoût

Makes 1¾ cups

½ pound wild mushrooms (lobster,
    chanterelle, morel or cèpes)
¼ cup thinly sliced ramps (whites only),
    green tops chiffonade and reserved
1 leek (white portion only), thinly sliced
1 shallot, thinly sliced
2 tablespoons vegetable oil
Salt and white pepper to taste
1 cup cold unsalted butter, cubed, *divided*
¼ cup white wine

In a mixing bowl, toss mushrooms, ramps,
leek and shallot with oil, salt and pepper.
Spread mixture onto a baking pan. Bake at
350° for 30 minutes or until mushrooms are
soft and tender and any excess liquid has
evaporated. Mushrooms can be stored
in a covered container for up to 2 days
before finishing.

To finish ragoût, heat 1 tablespoon butter in
a large cast-iron sauté pan over medium-
high heat. Add mushroom mixture; sauté
until heated through. Deglaze pan with
wine; reduce by half. Remove from the heat;
swirl in remaining cold butter until creamy.
Stir in green ramp tops. Adjust seasoning.

ᛐ

Duck Confit

Makes 2 cups

4 duck quarters (legs and thighs)
1 tablespoon kosher salt
1 tablespoon black peppercorns
4 sprigs thyme
4 cloves garlic, shaved
1 tablespoon juniper berries
2 bay leaves
2 shallots, sliced
2 cups rendered duck fat or extra virgin
    olive oil

Place duck in a square baking dish with
high sides; season liberally with salt. Add
peppercorns, thyme, garlic, juniper berries,
bay leaves and shallots; toss. Cover and
refrigerate overnight.

Remove dish from refrigerator. Cover duck
with duck fat, plastic wrap and foil. Bake
at 250° for 4 to 4½ hours or until meat is
falling off the bones. Allow duck to cool in
the fat. (When fully submerged in fat, duck
quarters can be preserved in the refrigerator
for up to 1 month.)

ᛐ

Chicken Stock

Makes 1¼ gallons

6½ pounds chicken bones

4 quarts cold water

2 quarts ice

2 cups chopped yellow onion

1 cup chopped celery

1 cup chopped carrot

1 head garlic, peeled and split

1 teaspoon dried thyme

2 bay leaves

1 tablespoon whole black peppercorns

1 cup white wine

Place bones in a large stockpot and cover with water. Bring to a simmer; skim any impurities that rise to the top. Turn off the heat and add ice to the stock; skim all fat that solidifies once all the ice has melted. Add remaining ingredients. Bring to a boil; reduce to a simmer for 45 minutes.

Periodically check stock and skim off fat that rises to the top. When finished, strain stock through a cheesecloth-lined fine mesh strainer. Discard bones and vegetables; reserve stock. Place in an ice-water bath until cool. Store in an airtight container in the refrigerator for up to 1 week, or freeze for up to 2 months.

For Duck Stock Prepare recipe as directed, using 6 pounds of duck bones.

For Rabbit Stock Prepare recipe as directed, using 6 pounds of rabbit bones.

For Chicken, Duck or Rabbit Demi-Glace

Makes 1½ cups

In a medium saucepan over medium-high heat, bring stock to a rolling boil. Reduce heat to a simmer; skim periodically and let stock reduce until thick enough to coat the back of a spoon. Strain through a fine mesh strainer. Adjust seasonings with salt and cider vinegar.

Veal Stock

Makes 2 quarts

10 pounds veal neck, back *and/or* shank bones

2 cups chopped yellow onion

1 cup chopped celery

1 cup chopped carrot

½ cup tomato purée

1 head garlic, peeled and split

1 teaspoon dried thyme

2 bay leaves

1 tablespoon black peppercorns

7 quarts cold water, divided

1 cup red wine

Place bones in a large roasting pan. Bake at 500° for 1½ hours until browned. Place onion, celery, carrot and tomato purée over bones. Continue browning, stirring occasionally, for 40 minutes. Use a slotted spoon to transfer bones and vegetables to a large stockpot. Add garlic, thyme, bay leaves and peppercorns.

Drain all the grease from the roasting pan. Add 1 quart of water to roasting pan; heat on the stove over medium heat. Scrape bottom of pan until all the drippings are loosened. Add drippings to stockpot. Add wine and remaining water. Bring to a boil; reduce heat to low and simmer for 6 hours.

Periodically check stock and skim off fat that rises to the top. When finished, strain stock through a cheesecloth-lined fine mesh strainer. Discard bones and vegetables; reserve stock. Refrigerate until completely cooled. Store in an airtight container in the refrigerator for up to 1 week, or freeze for up to 2 months.

For Beef Stock Prepare recipe as directed, using 10 pounds of beef bones.

For Game Stock Prepare recipe as directed, using 10 pounds of game bones such as venison or elk.

For Veal, Beef or Game Demi-Glace

Makes 2 cups

In a medium saucepan over medium-high heat, bring stock to a rolling boil. Reduce heat to a simmer; skim periodically and let stock reduce until thick enough to coat the back of a spoon. Strain twice through a fine mesh strainer. Adjust seasoning with salt and cider vinegar.

Shrimp Stock

Makes 2 quarts

2¼ cups packed shrimp shells
2 quarts cold water
1 cup chopped yellow onion
½ cup chopped celery
½ cup chopped carrot
1 teaspoon dried thyme
2 bay leaves
1 tablespoon black peppercorns
1 cup white wine

Place shells in a large stockpot and cover with water. Add remaining ingredients. Bring to a boil; reduce heat and simmer for 30 minutes. Skim any impurities and strain stock through a cheesecloth-lined fine mesh strainer. Discard shells and vegetables; reserve stock. Place in an ice-water bath until cool. Store in an airtight container in the refrigerator for up to 4 days, or freeze for up to 2 months.

ᛐ

Creole Brown Roux

Makes 3 cups

2 cups vegetable oil
3 cups all-purpose flour
⅓ cup minced yellow onion
⅓ cup minced green bell pepper
⅓ cup minced celery
1 teaspoon minced garlic

In a heavy 4- to 6-quart saucepan, being careful, bring the oil to the smoke point. Add flour, ¼ cup at a time, letting it get a dark, nutty brown before the next addition. Stir continuously so the flour doesn't burn.

When all of the flour is in and mixture is a nice brown color, remove from the heat. Stir in the remaining ingredients. This will start to cool off the roux, bring out more color and add flavor. Transfer roux to a bowl or container; when cool, refrigerate until ready to use. (Some of the oil will come to the top; mix it back in before using the roux.)

ᛐ

Poached Eggs

Makes 4

2 quarts water
6 tablespoons distilled vinegar
4 eggs
Ice water

In a stockpot over medium-high heat, bring water and vinegar to a simmer. Crack each egg into a small cup and carefully slide egg into poaching water. Cook for 2-3 minutes or until whites are set and opaque and yolks are still soft. With a slotted spoon, transfer eggs to a shallow pan filled with ice water. When ready to serve, reheat poached eggs in hot water until yolk runs hot, about 2 minutes.

ᛐ

Cornbread

Serves 8-12

$2/3$ cup all-purpose flour

$1/3$ cup cornmeal

$1/4$ cup corn flour *or* masa harina

$1/4$ cup sugar, optional

$2\frac{1}{2}$ teaspoons baking powder

Pinch salt

$2/3$ cup whole milk

2 eggs, lightly beaten

$2\frac{1}{2}$ tablespoons unsalted butter, melted

In a large bowl, combine the dry ingredients. In another bowl, combine the milk, eggs and butter. Pour over dry ingredients and stir until combined. Pour into a greased 8-inch square baking pan. Bake at 375° for 20 minutes or until a toothpick inserted in the center comes out clean.

Simple Syrup

Makes 4 cups

$2\frac{2}{3}$ cups water

$1\frac{2}{3}$ cups granulated sugar

$2/3$ cup light corn syrup

In a saucepan, combine all ingredients. Bring to a boil over high heat. Once the mixture comes to a boil, remove from the heat and cool. Can be stored in a covered container for 1 month in the refrigerator.

Source Guide

Most of the food items used in the recipes in this cookbook can be found at specialty grocery stores. Whole Foods Market, which has locations nationwide, is also a good source. In Texas, visit HEB's Central Market. We also recommend searching out farmers markets in your area ... find locations in Houston at www.urbanharvest.org and www.houstonfarmersmarket.org.

Butcher Supply

Allied Kenco Sales
26 Lyerly
Houston TX 77022
800.356.5189
www.alliedkenco.com

Fresh Gulf Seafood

Airline Seafood
1841 Richmond Avenue
Houston TX 77098
713.526.2351
Contact Steve Berreth

Seafood

Lobster Place
436 West 16th Street
New York NY 10011
212.255.5672
www.lobsterplace.com

Caviar

Petrossian Inc.
800.828.9241
www.petrossian.com

Gulf Shrimp

Texas Shrimp
877-TXCATCH (877.892.2824)
www.txshrimp.org

Quail, Pheasant, Chukar

Barrett's Quail Farm
12102 Westgard Boulevard
Houston TX 77044
281.458.2493

Pork

Berkshire Meats Inc.
75 East Main
Geneva MN 56035
507.256.7231
www.berkshiremeats.com

Antelope, Wild Boar, Venison

Broken Arrow Ranch
3296 Junction Highway
Ingram TX 78025
800.962.4263
www.brokenarrowranch.com

Demi-Glace, All Meats

Gourmet Ranch
800.775.0585
www.gourmetranch.com

Organic and Specialty Vegetables

Animal Farm Organic Garden
17623 Sycamore Road
Cat Spring TX 78933
979.992.3038

Peaches

Cooper Farms
185 County Road 1161
Fairfield TX 75840
903.389.2696
www.cooperfarmspeaches.com

Local Fruit and Vegetables

Froberg Farms
11875 County Road 190
Alvin TX 77511
281.585.3531

Mayhaws

Jackson's Fruit Farm
Livingston TX 77351
936.685.4658
jfarms@samlink.com

Local Tomatoes October to May

(delivery in Houston and at the farm on Saturdays)
M & R Hydroponic Farms
1811 McCales Road
Montgomery TX 77316
832.563.8543
Contact Michael Pierce
www.mrhydro.com

Wild and Foraged Vegetables

Truffles, mushrooms, ramps

Mikuni Wild Harvest

866.993.9927

www.mikuniwildharvest.com

Micro Greens, Pea Shoots

Wood Duck Farm

270 Pine Valley Road

Cleveland TX 77328

281.592.8774

www.woodduckfarm.com

Blue Corn Flour,
Carolina Gold Rice

Anson Mills

1922-C Gervais Street

Columbia SC 29201

803.467.4122

www.ansonmills.com

Honey and Honeycomb

Coplin Bee Farms

17726 Elizabeth Road

Algoa TX 77511

409.925.5415

Local Specialty Dry Goods
Chocolates, Spices

Euro-Mid Ltd.

1110 Seamist Drive

Houston TX 77008

713.880.1900

Popcorn Rice

Falcon Rice Mill Inc.

600 S. Avenue D

Crowley LA 70527-0771

800.738.7423

www.falconrice.com

Sriracha Hot Chili Sauce

Huy Fong Food Inc.

5001 Earle Avenue

Rosemead CA 91770

626.286.8328

www.huyfong.com

Olive Oil

Long Meadow Ranch Winery

1775 Whitehall Lane

St. Helena CA 94574

707.963.4555

www.longmeadowranch.com

Shiner Bock Beer

Shiner Brewing Co.

603 Brewery

Shiner TX 77989

www.shiner.com

Sugarcane Syrup,
Sugarcane Vinegar

Steen's Syrup

119 North Main Street

Abbeville LA 70510

800.725.1654

www.steensyrup.com

Acknowledgments

To all the guests who have made our Kitchen Table possible.

—

To the farmers and purveyors for their hard work so Brennan's can be supplied with the finest ingredients.

—

To my staff, which takes pride in creating great memories for our guests.

—

To all the chefs and sous chefs I've worked with through the years — you have influenced and enriched my career.

—

To the Brennan family, who gave a young cook a chance to learn and grow.

—

To Christy and Jay, who made this book look like it does.

—

To Kathryne, who made it happen.

—

To Alex and Carl for their unyielding support through this process.

—

To my family, who taught me hard work does pay off.

—

To Melanie, who supports me through every endeavor.

About Our Testers and How the Recipes Were Tested

From the onset, my goal for this book was to have recipes that certainly tested your skills as a cook, but ones that worked. Starting out as an amateur cook, I know nothing was more irritating than making a recipe and having the final outcome look nothing like the photo next to it.

Once all the recipes were compiled and in working order, my sous chefs and I went about testing the recipes on commercial equipment. The next step was to have the recipes retested by home cooks in a home environment on residential equipment. I enlisted three ladies, Melissa Ayers, Wendy Marciante and Mary Raybould, who have a passion for cooking and varying degrees of cooking experience.

Without their dedication, this book would never have happened. All three had been "Chef for a Day," so we were comfortable with each other. This comfort level allowed them to speak freely in regard to the recipes. We thought it would be difficult to assess the quality of the recipes with the ladies testing in their homes, so the only alternative was to test at Brennan's.

We brought the home kitchen to Brennan's, using a Jenn-Air gas stove with a gas-fired oven. I highly recommend the use of gas in the kitchen for immediate control, but if only electric is available, remember cooking times may need a little adjustment.

Heavy pans such as Le Creuset and copper were used for all stocks, soups and sauces. I recommend black French steel sauté pans for searing. The steel pans function much like cast-iron without the fear of cracking from overheating. Eventually the pan will season itself to be nearly nonstick.

The recipes were tested using the finest of ingredients, fresh seafood, meat and produce. Use the Source Guide on page 204 to find products not available in your local grocery store.

For the basic ingredients, we used large eggs, unsalted butter, all-purpose flour, granulated sugar, fresh herbs, kosher salt and freshly ground pepper, unless otherwise specified. Use cottonseed oil in place of vegetable oil for its mild flavor and high smoking point.

An instructor from culinary school used to say, "Garbage in, garbage out." That is certainly true; it is much easier to produce an unbelievable plate when you start with the finest ingredients available. The finest doesn't necessarily mean most expensive. Purchase local and seasonally when prices are lower due to a higher supply.

Be confident in yourself and the recipe. Remember to read and understand the recipe fully before attempting to make it; a second reading may be necessary. Don't fret … some of the recipes are advanced, but they can and have been prepared by amateur cooks.

Use your imagination and let this book be the jump start you need to create your own dish. Mix and match recipes; the sides and sauces can be used with other ingredients.

And most of all, have fun!

Recipe Index

LAGNIAPPE

Brennan's Brunch Hussard, 22

Smoked Catfish Mousse with
    Sweet Potato Chips, 25

Shrimp Beignets with Mirliton Relish, 26

Creole Gravlax with Seafood Boil
    Potato Salad, 28

Tempura Crab-Stuffed Squash Blossoms, 30

Crawfish Maque Choux with Jalapeño
    Corn Pound Cake, 33

SOUP

Oysters Rockefeller Soup, 38

Brennan's Gazpacho, 39

Cream of Sweet Corn Soup
    with Wild Mushrooms, 41

Gumbo Z'herbs with Cornmeal
    Drop Biscuits, 42

Smoked Chicken and Watercress
    Soup, 44

Crawfish Tortilla Soup, 45

Red Beans and Rice Soup, 46

Texas Shelling Pea and Beef Stew, 49

Sweet Potato Soup, 50

SALAD

Tuna Niçoise Salad, 54

Heirloom Tomato Salad, 55

Asparagus Hearts of Palm Salad, 57

Warm Spinach Salad, 58

Duck Confit Bistro Salad, 60

Texas Strawberry Salad, 62

Texas Peach Salad, 63

Homegrown Tomato Sundae
    with Meyer Lemon Olive Oil
    Ice Cream, 64

Berkshire Pork Tenderloin Salad, 66

CHARCUTERIE

Honey-Cured Bacon, 71

Tasso Ham, 73

Wild Boar Terrine, 74

Lamb and Rosemary Sausage, 76

Pancetta, 77

Cider-Poached Foie Gras Torchon, 78

Satsuma Orange Jelly, 81

Prickly Pear Jelly, 81

Satsuma Marmalade, 82

Texas Peach Preserves, 82

Mayhaw Jelly, 84

Venison and Shiner Bock Sliders, 86

Jalapeño Bread-and-Butter Pickles, 89

SEAFOOD

Halibut Provençal, 92

Grilled Tuna with Homegrown Tomatoes, 93

Lobster Américaine, 94

Peanut-Crusted Soft-Shell Crab, 98

Pan-Seared American Red Snapper
    with Gold Bar Squash Gratin
    and Crabmeat-Tarragon Sauce, 100

Blue Nose Bass with Cauliflower Purée, 102

Crawfish Sauce Piquant, 104

Jumbo Lump Crab Cakes with
    Sweet Corn Leek Sauce, 106

Wild Texas Shrimp with
    "Biscuits and Gravy", 109

Columbia River Sturgeon with
    Butternut Squash Hash, 111

MEAT

Lamb with Mustard Greens
    and Cornbread Custard, 114

Sika Venison with Texas Field Pea
    Fricassee and Bacon-Corn
    Johnnycakes, 116

Veal "Wellington", 120

Truffle-Scented Poussin with Rutabaga
    and Chestnut Hash, 122

Duck Pot Pie, 124

Texas Bobwhite Quail with Honey-Balsamic
    Gastrique and Apple-Beet Salad, 126

Black Lacquered Duck
    with Foie Gras Bombe, 128

Rabbit Three Ways with Barley Risotto, 130

Confit of Berkshire Pork
    with Sweet Potato Spaetzle, 133

Southern Comfort Short Ribs
    with Pork and Beans, 137

Cocoa Nib-Crusted Châteaubriand with
    Blue Cheese Lyonnaise Potatoes, 138

CHEESE

Purple Haze Soufflé, 143

Fleur-de-Lis Fromage Triple Cream
    Cheese with Petrossian Caviar
    and Blue Corn Blini, 145

Ewe's Blue with Seckle Pear, 146

Brûlée of Appalachian Jack, 148

Boere Kaas Super Aged
    Gouda Fondue, 148

DESSERT

Chocolate S'mores, 152

Bit-o-Honey Beehives with
    Texas Honey Ice Cream, 154

Chilled Strawberry Basil Soup
    with Champagne Sorbet, 156

Rustic Tart with Vanilla Bean Crust
    and Sugarcane-Pecan Ice Cream, 159

Brennan's Peanut Butter Cup, 161

Peach Upside-Down Cakes with
    Peach Ice Cream, 165

Vanilla Bean Pound Cake with
    Praline Ice Cream, 166

Meyer Lemon Mini Spice Cakes
    with Meyer Lemon Sherbet, 168

Popcorn Rice Crème Caramel, 171

Creole Cream Cheese Crêpes
    with Texas Strawberries, 172

OPEN KITCHEN NIGHT

Drunken Watermelon Margarita, 176

Brandy Crusta, 176

Milk and Cookies: Molasses Sugar Cookies
    and Brandy Milk Punch, 179

Mint Julep Moderne, 180

Pomegranate Daiquiri, 180

Creole Martini with
    Crab-Stuffed Olives, 181

Pecan-Crusted Cabrito Lollipops, 183

Sno-Cones: Blueberry Meyer
    Lemon Martini, Mango Mojito,
    Mardi Gras Hurricane, 184

Open-Faced Venison Reubens, 186

Duck Confit Poppers, 191

THE PANTRY

Creole Meat and Seafood Seasoning, 198

Ravigote Sauce, 198

Rémoulade Sauce, 198

Creole Tomato Sauce, 199

Seafood Boil, 199

Spiced Peanuts and Pecans, 199

Olive Tapenade, 200

Wild Mushroom Ragoût, 200

Duck Confit, 200

Stock — Beef, Chicken, Duck, Game,
    Rabbit, Shrimp and Veal, 201 and 202

Demi-Glace — Beef, Chicken, Duck,
    Game, Rabbit and Veal, 201

Creole Brown Roux, 202

Poached Eggs, 202

Cornbread, 203

Simple Syrup, 203

A

Almonds, Candied, 62

American Red Snapper, Pan-Seared, 100

Américaine, Lobster, 94

Américaine, Sauce, 94

Appalachian Jack, Brûlée of, 148

Appetizers

    Brennan's Brunch Hussard, 22

    Crawfish Maque Choux with

        Jalapeño Corn Pound Cake, 33

    Ewe's Blue with Seckle Pear, 146

    Fleur-de-Lis Fromage Triple Cream

        Cheese with Petrossian Caviar, 145

    Foie Gras Bombe, 128

    Jumbo Lump Crab Cakes, 106

    Purple Haze Soufflé, 143

    Tempura Crab-Stuffed Squash

        Blossoms, 30

Apple-Beet Salad, 127

Apple-Pecan Confiture, 148

Art and science of seasoning, 197

Artisan cheese makers, 147

Asparagus Hearts of Palm Salad, 57

B

Bacon-Corn Johnnycakes, 116

Bacon Dressing, 60

Bacon, Honey-Cured, 71

Barley Risotto, 130

Basil Oil, 156

Bass, Blue Nose with Cauliflower

  Purée, 102

Beans, Pork and, 137

Beans, Red Bean Soup, 46

Beef

    Demi-Glace, 201

    Cocoa Nib-Crusted Châteaubriand,

        138

    Southern Comfort Short Ribs, 137

    Stew with Shelling Peas, 49

    Stock, 201

Beignets, Shrimp, 26

Berkshire Pork Tenderloin Salad, 66

Beverages (see Drinks and Cocktails)

Biscuits

    Buttermilk, 109

    Buttermilk Pudding, 109

    Cornmeal Drop, 42

Bit-o-Honey Beehives, 154

Black Lacquered Duck, 128

Blini, Blue Corn, 145

Blue Cheese Lyonnaise Potatoes, 138

Blueberry Meyer Lemon Martini, 184

Bobwhite Quail with Honey-Balsamic

  Gastrique, 126

Boere Kaas Super Aged Gouda

  Fondue, 148

Boudin, Shrimp, 26

Brandy Crusta, 176

Brandy Milk Punch, 179

Bread-and-Butter Pickles, 89

Brennan's Brunch Hussard, 22

Brennan's Gazpacho, 39

Brennan's Peanut Butter Cup, 161

Brûlée of Appalachian Jack, 148

Butternut Squash Hash, 111

C

Cabbage Slaw, Savoy, 133

Cabrito, Pecan-Crusted Lollipops, 183

Cake

    Jalapeño Corn Pound Cake, 33

    Meyer Lemon Mini Spice Cakes, 168

    Peach Upside-Down Cakes, 165

    Spongecake, 154

    Vanilla Bean Pound Cake, 166

Candied Almonds, 62

Candied Citrus Zest, 168

Candied Pecans, 63

Canning, method, 85

Catfish, Smoked Mousse, 25

Cauliflower Purée, 102

Caviar, American Sturgeon, 145

Celeriac-Apple Salad, 95

Champagne Sorbet, 156

Châteaubriand, Cocoa-Nib Crusted, 138

Cheese

    Blue Cheese Lyonnaise

        Potatoes, 138

    Boere Kaas Super Aged

        Gouda Fondue, 148

    Brûlée of Appalachian Jack, 148

    Creole Cream Cheese, 172

    Ewe's Blue with Seckle Pear, 146

    Fleur-de-Lis Fromage Triple Cream

        Cheese, 145

    Heirloom Tomato Salad, 55

    Purple Haze Soufflé, 143

Cheese makers, list of, 147

Cheese plate, creating your own, 142

Chicken
    Demi-Glace, 201
    Stock, 201
    Smoked Chicken and Watercress
      Soup, 44
    Truffle-Scented Poussin with
    Rutabaga Hash, 122
Chilled Strawberry Basil Soup, 156
Chive Oil, 92
Chocolate, Ganache, 161
Chocolate, Peanut Butter Cup, 161
Chocolate S'mores, 152
Cider-Poached Foie Gras Torchon, 78
Columbia River Sturgeon with Butternut
  Hash, 111
Cocktails
    Blueberry Meyer Lemon Martini, 184
    Brandy Crusta, 176
    Brandy Milk Punch, 179
    Creole Martini with Crab-Stuffed
      Olives, 181
    Drunken Watermelon Margarita, 176
    Mango Mojito, 184
    Mardi Gras Hurricane, 185
    Mint Julep Moderne, 180
    Pomegranate Daiquiri, 180
    Sno-Cones, 184

Confit
    Berkshire Pork, 133
    Duck, 200
    Duck Poppers, 191
    Duck Bistro Salad, 60
    Rabbit, 130
    Yellow and Red Tomato, 92

Cookies, Molasses Sugar, 179
Cornbread, 203
Cornbread Custard, 114
Cornmeal Drop Biscuits, 42
Coulis, Red Pepper, 66
Crab
    Crabmeat-Tarragon Sauce, 101
    Jumbo Lump Crab Cakes, 106
    Peanut-Crusted Soft-Shell, 98
    Stuffed Olives, 181
    Stuffed Squash Blossoms, 30
Crawfish
    Maque Choux, 33
    Sauce Piquant, 104
    Tortilla Soup, 45
Creamed Mustard Greens, 114
Creamy Cilantro Dressing, 191
Crème Fraîche, Sweetened, 172
Creole Brown Roux, 202
Creole Gravlax with a Boil Salad, 28
Creole Martini with Crab-Stuffed
    Olives, 181
Creole Meat Seasoning, 198
Creole Mustard-Orange Gastrique, 183
Creole Seafood Seasoning, 198
Creole Tomato Sauce, 199
Crêpes, Creole Cream Cheese, 172
Curry, Sweet Red Vinaigrette, 30

D
Daiquiri, Pomegranate, 180
Demi-Glace
    Beef, 201
    Chicken, 201
    Duck, 201
    Game, 201
    Jack Daniels Creole Mustard, 114
    Marsala, 121
    Perigord Chicken, 122
    Rabbit, 201
    Satsuma-Chicory, 128
    Steen's Sugarcane Barbecue, 133
    Veal, 201
Desserts
    Bit-o-Honey Beehives, 154
    Brennan's Peanut Butter Cup, 161
    Chilled Strawberry Basil Soup, 156
    Chocolate S'mores, 152
    Creole Cream Cheese Crêpes
      with Texas Strawberries, 172
    Meyer Lemon Mini Spice Cakes, 168
    Milk and Cookies, 179
    Molasses Sugar Cookies, 179
    Peach Upside-Down Cakes, 165
    Popcorn Rice Crème Caramel, 171
    Rustic Tart with Vanilla Bean
      Crust, 159
    Vanilla Bean Pound Cake
      with Praline Ice Cream, 166
Dressings (see Salad Dressings)

Drinks
    Blueberry Meyer Lemon Martini, 184
    Brandy Crusta, 176
    Brandy Milk Punch, 179
    Creole Martini with Crab-Stuffed
       Olives, 181
    Drunken Watermelon Margarita, 176
    Mango Mojito, 184
    Mardi Gras Hurricane, 185
    Mint Julep Moderne, 180
    Pomegranate Daiquiri, 180
    Sno-Cones, 184
Drunken Watermelon Margarita, 176
Dry rub for pork, 66
Duck
    Black Lacquered Duck, 128
    Confit Bistro Salad, 60
    Confit Poppers, 191
    Demi-Glace, 201
    Pot Pie, 124
    Stock, 201

E

Eggs
    Brennan's Brunch Hussard, 22
    Fried Poached, 57
    Poached, 202
    Purple Haze Soufflé, 143
Entrées
    Black Lacquered Duck, 128
    Blue Nose Bass with
       Cauliflower Purée, 102
    Brennan's Brunch Hussard, 22

Cocoa Nib-Crusted
    Châteaubriand, 138
Columbia River Sturgeon with
    Butternut Hash, 111
Confit of Berkshire Pork with
    Sweet Potato Spaetzle, 133
Crawfish Sauce Piquant, 104
Duck Pot Pie, 124
Grilled Tuna with Homegrown
    Tomatoes, 93
Halibut Provençal, 92
Jumbo Lump Crab Cakes, 106
Lamb with Mustard Greens and
    Cornbread Custard, 114
Lobster Américaine, 94
Pan-Seared American Red
    Snapper, 100
Peanut-Crusted Soft-Shell Crab, 98
Rabbit Three Ways, 130
Sika Venison with Texas Field
    Pea Fricassee, 116
Southern Comfort Short Ribs with
    Pork and Beans, 137
Texas Bobwhite Quail with Honey-
    Balsamic Gastrique, 126
Truffle-Scented Poussin with
    Rutabaga Hash, 122
Veal "Wellington", 120
Wild Texas Shrimp with "Biscuits
    and Gravy", 109

F

Fennel Sauerkraut, 186
Field Pea Fricassee, 116
Fish
    Blue Nose Bass, 102
    Columbia River Sturgeon, 111
    Creole Gravlax, 28
    Grilled Tuna, 93
    Halibut Provençal, 92
    Pan-Seared American Red
       Snapper, 100
    Smoked Catfish Mousse, 25
    Tuna Niçoise Salad, 54
Foie Gras
    Bombe, 128
    Cider-Poached Torchon, 78
    Cleaning of, 194
    Preparing a torchon, 79
    Veal "Wellington", 120
Fondue, Boere Kaas Super Aged
    Gouda, 148
Fried Green Tomatoes, 22
Fried Poached Eggs, 57
Fruit
    Apple-Beet Salad, 127
    Apple-Pecan Confiture, 148
    Celeriac-Apple Salad, 95
    Chilled Strawberry Basil Soup, 156
    Ewe's Blue with Seckle Pear, 146
    Texas Peach Salad, 63
    Texas Strawberry Salad, 62

G

Game (also see Duck and Venison)
  Bobwhite Quail, 126
  Demi-Glace, 201
  Stock, 201
  Rabbit Three Ways, 130
  Wild Boar Terrine, 74
Ganache, 161
Gastrique, Creole Mustard-Orange, 183
Gazpacho, Brennan's, 39
Gratin, Gold Bar Squash, 100
Gravlax, Creole, 28
Grilled Tuna with Homegrown
  Tomatoes, 93
Grilled Vegetables, 66
Gumbo Z'herbs, 42

H

Halibut Provençal, 92
Ham, Tasso, 73
Hash, Butternut Squash, 111
Hash, Rutabaga and Chestnut, 122
Heirloom Tomato Salad, 55
Homegrown Tomato Sundae, 64
Honey-Cured Bacon, 71
Hors D'oeuvres
  Brûlée of Appalachian Jack, 148
  Boere Kaas Super Aged Gouda
    Fondue, 148
  Creole Gravlax with a Boil
    Salad, 28

Duck Confit Poppers, 191
  Open-Faced Venison Reubens, 186
  Pecan-Crusted Cabrito
    Lollipops, 183
  Shrimp Beignets, 26
  Smoked Catfish Mousse, 25
Hurricane, Mardi Gras, 185
Hussard, Brennan's Brunch, 22

I

Ice Cream
  Meyer Lemon Olive Oil, 64
  Peach, 165
  Peanut Butter, 161
  Praline, 166
  Sugarcane-Pecan, 159
  Texas Honey, 154
Ingredient Close-Ups
  Balsamic vinegar, 65
  Canning and preserving, 85
  Cleaning foie gras, 194
  Curing meats, 70
  Edible mushrooms, 51
  Game, 119
  Grading tuna, 103
  Gulf shrimp, 27
  Preparing a foie gras torchon, 79
  Prepping a soft-shell crab, 195

J

Jack Daniels Creole Mustard
  Demi-Glace, 114
Jackson Dressing, 54
Jalapeño Bread-and-Butter Pickles, 89
Jalapeño Corn Pound Cake, 33
Jelly
  Mayhaw, 84
  Prickly Pear, 81
  Satsuma Orange, 81
Johnnycakes, Bacon-Corn, 116
Julep, Mint Moderne, 180
Jumbo Lump Crab Cakes, 106

L

Lamb
  and Rosemary Sausage, 76
  with Mustard Greens and Cornbread
    Custard, 114
Lemon
  Mini Spice Cakes, 168
  Olive Oil Ice Cream, 64
  Sherbet, 168
Lemongrass Vinaigrette, 98
Lobster Américaine, 94
Louisiana Popcorn Rice, 104
Lyonnaise Potatoes, Blue Cheese, 138

M

Mango Mojito, 184

Maque Choux, Crawfish, 33

Marchands de Vin Sauce, 22

Mardi Gras Hurricane, 185

Margarita, Drunken Watermelon, 176

Marinade, Southern Comfort, 137

Marmalade, Satsuma, 82

Marsala Demi-Glace, 121

Martini, Creole, 181

Mayhaw Jelly, 84

Meat, curing of, 70

Meat Seasoning, Creole, 198

Meringue, Italian, 155

Milk and Cookies, 179

Mint Julep Moderne, 180

Mirliton Relish, 26

Mirliton Slaw, 106

Molasses Sugar Cookies, 179

Mornay Sauce, 100

Mousse

    Chocolate, 152

    Peanut Butter, 161

    Smoked Catfish, 25

Mushroom

    Charred Wild Mushrooms, 58

    Edible varieties of, 51

    Stock, 49

    Wild Mushroom Ragoût, 200

    Wild Mushroom Sauté, 41

Mustard Greens, Creamed, 114

N

Niçoise Salad, Tuna, 54

Nuts

    Candied Almonds, 62

    Candied Pecans, 63

    Peanut Brittle, 161

    Spiced Peanuts, 199

    Spiced Pecans, 199

O

Oil

    Basil, 156

    Chive, 92

Olive Tapenade, 200

Olives, Crab-Stuffed, 181

Open-Faced Venison Reubens, 186

Orange Jelly, Satsuma, 81

Oysters Rockefeller Soup, 38

P

Pancetta, 77

Pan-Seared American Red Snapper, 100

Peach

    Ice Cream, 165

    Preserves, 82

    Salad, 63

    Upside-Down Cakes, 165

Peanut/Peanut Butter

    Brittle, 161

    Crusted Soft-Shell Crab, 98

    Cup, Brennan's, 161

    Ice Cream, 161

    Mousse, 161

    Spiced, 199

Pecan-Crusted Cabrito Lollipops, 183

Pecans, Spiced, 199

Perigord Chicken Demi-Glace, 122

Pickles

    Bread-and-Butter, 89

    Jalapeño Bread-and-Butter, 89

Poached Eggs, 202

Poached Eggs, Fried, 57

Pomegranate Daiquiri, 180

Popcorn Rice Crème Caramel, 171

Popcorn Rice, Louisiana, 104

Poppers, Duck Confit, 191

Pork

    and Beans, 137

    Berkshire Confit, 133

    Berkshire Tenderloin Salad, 66

    Dry Rub, 66

    Honey-Cured Bacon, 71

    Pancetta, 77

    Tasso Ham, 73

Potato Salad, Seafood Boil, 28

Potatoes, Blue Cheese Lyonnaise, 138

Pot Pie, Duck, 124

Poussin, Truffle-Scented, 122

Punch, Brandy Milk, 179

Purple Haze Soufflé, 143

Praline Ice Cream, 166

Preserves, Texas Peach, 82

Prickly Pear Jelly, 81

Puff Pastry

    Duck Pot Pie, 124

    Lobster Américaine, 94

    Shrimp Beignets, 26

    Veal "Wellington", 120

Q

Quail, Bobwhite with Honey-Balsamic
　　Gastrique, 126

R

Rabbit
　　Braised, 130
　　Confit, 130
　　Demi-Glace, 201
　　Rack of, 130
　　Stock, 201
Ragoût, Wild Mushroom, 200
Raisins, Rum, 171
Ravigote Sauce, 198
Red Beans and Rice Soup, 46
Red Pepper Coulis, 66
Red Snapper, Pan-Seared, 100
Relish
　　Mirliton, 26
　　Wild Rice, 46
Rémoulade Sauce, 198
Reubens, Open-Faced Venison, 186
Rice
　　and Red Bean Soup, 46
　　Crème Caramel Popcorn, 171
　　Louisiana Popcorn, 104
Risotto, Barley, 130
Rolls, Silver Dollar, 86
Roux, Creole Brown, 202
Rub, dry for pork, 66
Russian Dressing, 186
Rustic Tart with Vanilla Bean Crust, 159
Rutabaga and Chestnut Hash, 122

S

Sage Butter Sauce, 111
Salad Dressings (also see Vinaigrettes)
　　Bacon, 60
　　Creamy Cilantro, 191
　　Dijon, 58
　　Jackson, 54
　　Russian, 186
Salads
　　Apple-Beet, 127
　　Asparagus Hearts of Palm, 57
　　Berkshire Pork Tenderloin, 66
　　Celeriac-Apple, 95
　　Duck Confit Bistro, 60
　　Ewe's Blue with Seckle Pear, 146
　　Fennel Sauerkraut, 186
　　Heirloom Tomato, 55
　　Homegrown Tomato Sundae, 64
　　Mirliton Slaw, 106
　　Savoy Cabbage Slaw, 133
　　Seafood Boil Potato, 28
　　Texas Peach, 63
　　Texas Strawberry, 62
　　Tuna Niçoise, 54
　　Warm Spinach, 58
Sandwiches
　　Open-Faced Venison Reubens, 186
　　Venison and Shiner Bock Sliders, 86
Satsuma-Chicory Demi-Glace, 128
Satsuma Marmalade, 82
Satsuma Orange Jelly, 81
Sauces (also see Demi-Glace)
　　SAVORY
　　Américaine, 94
　　Crabmeat-Tarragon, 101

Creole Mustard-Orange
　　Gastrique, 183
Creole Tomato, 199
Marchands de Vin, 22
Mornay, 100
Ravigote, 198
Red Pepper Coulis, 66
Rémoulade, 198
Sage Butter, 111
Sweet Corn Leek, 106
SWEET
Caramel, 166
Ganache, 161
Strawberry, 172
Sausage
　　Lamb and Rosemary, 76
　　Shrimp Boudin, 26
　　Venison and Shiner Bock, 86
Savoy Cabbage Slaw, 133
Sauerkraut, Fennel, 186
Scallops
　　Blue Nose Bass with
　　　Cauliflower Purée,102
　　Brennan's Gazpacho, 39
Seafood (see Crab, Crawfish, Fish,
　Tuna, Scallops, Shrimp)
Seafood Boil, 199
Seafood Boil Potato Salad, 28
Seasoning, art and science of, 197
Seasonings
　　Creole Meat, 198
　　Creole Seafood, 198
　　Pork Dry Rub, 66
Tasso, 73

Sherbet, Meyer Lemon, 168

Short Ribs, Southern Comfort, 137

Shrimp

    Beignets, 26

    Boudin, 26

    Wild Texas Shrimp with "Biscuits
      and Gravy", 109

Side Dishes

    Bacon-Corn Johnnycakes, 116

    Barley Risotto, 130

    Blue Cheese Lyonnaise
      Potatoes, 138

    Buttermilk Biscuit Pudding, 109

    Butternut Squash Hash, 111

    Cauliflower Purée, 102

    Cornbread Custard, 114

    Creamed Mustard Greens, 114

    Foie Gras Bombe, 128

    Fried Green Tomatoes, 22

    Gold Bar Squash Gratin, 100

    Grilled Vegetables, 66

    Louisiana Popcorn Rice, 104

    Pork and Beans, 137

    Rutabaga and Chestnut Hash, 122

    Sweet Potato Spaetzle, 133

    Texas Field Pea Fricassee, 116

Sika Venison, 116

Silver Dollar Rolls, 86

Simple Syrup, 203

Sliders, Venison, 86

Smoked Catfish Mousse, 25

Smoked Chicken and Watercress Soup, 44

S'mores, Chocolate, 152

Sno-Cones, 184

Soft-Shell Crab, Peanut-Crusted, 98

Soft-shell crab, prepping of, 195

Sorbet, Champagne, 156

Soufflé, Purple Haze, 143

Soups

    Brennan's Gazpacho, 39

    Chilled Strawberry Basil, 156

    Crawfish Tortilla, 45

    Cream of Sweet Corn
      with Wild Mushrooms, 41

    Gumbo Z'herbs, 42

    Oysters Rockefeller, 38

    Red Beans and Rice, 46

    Smoked Chicken and Watercress, 44

    Sweet Potato, 50

Source Guide, 204

Southern Comfort Marinade, 137

Spiced Peanuts, 199

Spiced Pecans, 199

Spinach Salad, Warm, 58

Squash

    Blossoms, Crab-Stuffed, 30

    Butternut Hash, 111

    Gold Bar Gratin, 100

Steen's Sugarcane Barbecue
   Demi-Glace, 133

Stew, Shelling Pea and Beef, 49

Stock

    Beef, 201

    Chicken, 201

    Court-Bouillon, 94

    Duck, 201

    Game, 201

    Mushroom, 49

    Rabbit, 201

    Seafood Boil, 199

    Shrimp, 202

    Veal, 201

Strawberry Basil Soup, 156

Strawberry Salad, 62

Sturgeon, Columbia River, 111

Sugarcane-Pecan Ice Cream, 159

Sugarcane, Steen's Barbecue
   Demi-Glace, 133

Sugarcane Vinaigrette, 93

Sweet Corn Leek Sauce, 106

Sweet Corn Soup, Cream of, 41

Sweet Potato

    Chips, 25

    Soup, 50

    Spaetzle, 133

Sweet Red Curry Vinaigrette, 30

T

Tapenade, Olive, 200

Tart, Rustic with Vanilla Bean Crust, 159

Tasso Ham, 73

Techniques and terms, 196

Tempura Batter, 30

Tempura Crab-Stuffed Squash Blossoms, 30

Terrine, Wild Boar, 74

Testing of recipes in this book, 207

Texas

    Field Pea Fricassee, 116

    Honey Ice Cream, 154

    Peach Preserves, 82

    Peach Salad, 63

    Peach Vinaigrette, 63

    Strawberry Salad, 62

    Strawberry Vinaigrette, 62

Tomato

    Creole Sauce, 199

    Fried Green, 22

    Heirloom Salad, 55

    Homegrown with Grilled Tuna, 93

    Gazpacho, 39

    Tomato Sundae, 64

    Yellow and Red Confit, 92

Torchon, Cider-Poached Foie Gras, 78

Torchon, steps for, 79

Trufffle Vinaigrette, 57

Tuile, Coconut Batter, 171

Tuna

    Grading of, 103

    Grilled with Homegrown
      Tomatoes, 93

    Niçoise Salad, 54

V

Veal

    Demi-Glace, 201

    Stock, 201

    "Wellington", 120

Vegetables, Grilled, 66

Venison

    and Shiner Bock Sliders, 86

    Open-Faced Reubens, 186

    with Texas Field Pea Fricassee, 116

Vinaigrettes (also see Salad Dressings)

    Dried Cherry, 146

    Lemongrass, 98

    Sugarcane, 93

    Sweet Red Curry, 30

    Texas Peach, 63

    Texas Strawberry, 62

    Truffle, 57

W

Warm Spinach Salad, 58

Watermelon, Drunken, 176

"Wellington", Veal, 120

Wild Boar Terrine, 74

Wild Texas Shrimp with "Biscuits
   and Gravy", 109

Thank you! Chris S.
9-20-05

There once was a man named "JUST 6 SPOONS + PASS
JOSE.   IT AROUND THE TAB
who brought us fine food on
Anne's special day.
Course after course arrived
our delights
We soon knew Brennan's
kitchen was outta sight
when desert finally came
with a cherry on top
we thought we had made
it
Except that we POPPED!